Salads

Salads

Over 140 recipes for simple and fresh dishes—perfect all year round

First published in 2010
LOVE FOOD is an imprint of Parragon Books Ltd

Parragon
Queen Street House
4 Queen Street
Bath BA1 1HE, UK

Copyright © Parragon Books Ltd 2010

LOVE FOOD and the accompanying heart device is a registered trademark of Parragon Books Ltd in Australia, the UK, and the EU.

ISBN: 978-1-4075-9302-9

Printed in China

Internal design by Simon Levy
New photography by Clive Bozzard-Hill
New home economy by Valerie Barrett
New recipes, introduction, and cover text by Angela Drake

Notes for the Reader
This book uses imperial, metric, and US cup measurements. Follow the same units of measurement throughout; do not mix imperial and metric. All spoon measurements are level: teaspoons are assumed to be 5 ml, and tablespoons are assumed to be 15 ml. Unless otherwise stated, milk is assumed to be whole, eggs and individual vegetables, such as potatoes, are medium, and pepper is freshly ground black pepper.

The times given are an approximate guide only. Preparation times differ according to the techniques used by different people and the cooking times may also vary from those given as a result of the type of oven used. Optional ingredients, variations, or serving suggestions have not been included in the calculations.

Recipes using raw or very lightly cooked eggs should be avoided by infants, the elderly, pregnant women, convalescents, and anyone with a chronic condition. Pregnant and breast-feeding women are advised to avoid eating peanuts and peanut products. People with nut allergies should be aware that some of the prepared ingredients used in the recipes in this book may contain nuts. Always check the packaging before use.

Vegetarians should be aware that some of the prepared ingredients used in the recipes in this book may contain animal products. Always check the packaging before use.

CONTENTS

6 Introduction

18 Meat

66 Poultry

118 Fish & Seafood

168 Vegetarian

216 Health-Boosting

266 Fruit

316 Index

INTRODUCTION

FULL OF GOODNESS

Gone are the days when the word "salad" conjured up the image of a few limp lettuce leaves on the side of your plate. Salads have really come of age with the most vibrant and exciting range of ingredients available to create sensational dishes to suit any occasion.

A quick stroll around even the smallest supermarket or grocers will reveal a cornucopia of fantastic salad ingredients, from peppery salad greens and fragrant herbs to colorful sun-ripened fruit and vegetables—so easy to transform into fresh and appetizing meals with minimum time and effort. Today, salads are the most versatile of dishes incorporating flavors from all around the world. Whether it's a traditional crisp Greek salad, a filling warm chicken and pasta salad, or an energy-boosting bean salad, you'll find the perfect salad to feed family and friends.

THE HEALTHY OPTION

The health benefits of regularly eating salads cannot be ignored. We all aspire to living a healthier lifestyle, and eating salads packed with nutritious leafy greens, vegetables, beans, herbs, nuts, and seeds will certainly boost your intake of protein and essential vitamins, minerals, and fiber. We are frequently reminded that a healthy diet includes eating a minimum of five portions of fruit and vegetables every day—tuck into a hearty salad for lunch or dinner or replace rice or potatoes with a tasty side salad and you will be well on the way to that target.

For those who are constantly having to watch their weight, this book will be a revelation. Not long ago anyone on a diet would stick to a simple, but very boring, virtually calorie-free salad of lettuce, tomato, cucumber, and celery with no dressing! Well, times have certainly changed. Choose carefully and you can still enjoy a thoroughly satisfying salad without piling on the pounds. Look for salads that have yogurt-base dressings, such as Sweet Potato Salad, or ones that are only lightly dressed, such as Wild Rice Salad with Cucumber & Orange or Minted Pea & Melon Salad.

However, don't be put off by the quantity of oil in many of the dressings. A healthy balanced diet needs to include a small amount of fat. Nut and vegetable oils (such as sunflower and olive oil) contain unsaturated fat, which can help to lower harmful cholesterol in the blood. Also, the fat in

some oils and oily fish, such as mackerel, contains the essential omega-3 or omega-6 fatty acids that are important for growth, healthy skin, and a strong immune system.

Grains and beans play an important role in a healthy diet and can release a steady supply of energy throughout the day. On hectic and energetic days, pick a fiber-packed salad, such as Three Bean Salad or Tabbouleh for lunch, and you'll find that hunger pangs are kept well at bay for a good few hours.

A SALAD FOR ALL SEASONS

It's not surprising that many of us think about eating or cooking salads only during the summer—salads are the perfect solution for easy-to-prepare meals when the days are long and hot. But salads really can be served all year around and in this book you'll find salads to suit all seasons, whatever the weather. We are no longer restricted by seasonal fluctuations for many ingredients and fresh produce can be flown all over the world. So you can enjoy most of the salads in this book all year round. However, it's always best to choose fresh homegrown produce when it's at its prime. Let's face it, nothing can beat the flavor of freshly dug new potatoes in a delicious creamy dressed potato salad—the ideal accompaniment for a sizzling summer barbecue or alfresco supper.

Springtime is one of the best times of the year for serving salads. Stores will be full to the brim with an abundance of crisp, young spring vegetables and seasonal salad greens. With days becoming longer and warmer, light and nutritious salads are the natural choices to boost our energy levels after the winter slump.

In the heat of summer, choose salads that are quick and easy to cook—no one wants to work away in a hot kitchen when they could be outdoors enjoying the good weather. For alfresco dinner parties, summer buffets, and barbecues, pick salads that can be made a few hours in advance, or prepare the separate elements of the salads and simply toss together just before serving.

During the colder months of the year opt for comforting and hearty warm salads or filling pasta or rice salads. Take time to marinate fish, meat, and poultry for extra flavor or slow roast vegetables with winter herbs and garlic. If you're entertaining, a salad can be the ideal light appetizer choice for a winter dinner party.

THE FINEST INGREDIENTS

Never before has there been such a huge range of salad ingredients to choose from. Here's a quick guide to some of the essentials.

SALAD GREENS

With an endless variety of shapes, textures, colors, and flavors, salad greens really do make or break a good salad. Leaves with a robust and peppery taste include frisée, arugula, mizuna, and watercress. For a salad with a milder taste, pick delicate mâche or a classic round butterhead. For the crispiest salad, you can't beat romaine or iceberg lettuces. To add extra color to a leafy salad, look for Swiss chard leaves with ruby red stalks, variegated oak leaf or lollo rosso leaves, or firm red chicory leaves.

Many of the recipes in this book suggest using bags of mixed salad greens and you'll find an ever-changing selection of leafy mixtures in most supermarkets. Quick to buy and very convenient, they are a boon to the busy cook. However, do check them for freshness because the leaves can deteriorate quickly. Don't worry if you can't find a specific salad bag for a recipe; simply substitute another one or buy separate greens and make up your own mix.

HERBS

Fragrant fresh herbs can bring an everyday salad to life. The classic Mediterranean herbs, such as basil, oregano, and flat-leaf parsley, are essentials for many salads and go particularly well with tomatoes, bell peppers, and onions. Cilantro and mint add an aromatic touch to Asian and Middle Eastern-themed salads, while delicate and feathery herbs, such as dill, fennel, and chervil, with their mild aniseed taste, suit fish and shellfish salads. More robust herbs with woody stalks, such as thyme and rosemary, are great for adding to marinades—simply bruise or break the stalks to release more flavor.

If you have space in the yard, it's worth growing your own herbs or planting a few in a window box or hanging basket for handy picking. Alternatively, buy pots of growing herbs and put them in a shaded spot on the kitchen windowsill and remember to water them regularly.

OILS

The basis of most salad dressings, the choice of a good-quality oil is vital to a successful salad. Extracted from various nuts, seeds, and beans, oils can vary in flavor from bland and virtually tasteless to highly aromatic and intensely rich.

Olive oil is by far the most popular oil to use in most dressings. Produced in hot Mediterranean countries, such as France, Greece, Italy, and Spain, the prized extra virgin olive oil is considered the finest. It has a dark green color and strong rich taste and is from the first cold pressing of olives. Use sparingly because it can be overpowering for some delicate salads. Milder and paler olive oils from further pressings may be more suitable for some recipes.

Nut oils also vary considerably in flavor and intensity. Peanut oil is a pale oil with a mild and nutty aroma. Walnut and hazelnut oils have wonderfully intense flavors but they can be expensive. Buy in small quantities and use within a few months of opening because they can soon go rancid.

Sesame seed oil is frequently used in Asian-themed salads. It has a deep amber color and a heady aroma with a really nutty taste. A few drops are all that's needed for most recipes.

Sunflower and corn oils both have a fairly mild, somewhat bland taste. Use them for dressings and marinades where other stronger flavorings will dominate, such as fresh herbs, garlic, or chile. They can also be blended with more expensive oils to dilute the intense flavor.

VINEGARS

The second essential element of a salad dressing is usually vinegar. Those distilled from wine—either white or red—are the most frequently used in salad dressings. Other vinegars, such as sherry and cider, are popular too and can be used to complement the ingredients in a salad. Mild and sweet cider vinegar goes particularly well with salads that contain fruit, while rich and nutty sherry vinegar is delicious with warm meat and poultry salads.

Balsamic vinegar comes from the Italian region of Modena and is a rich, yet mellow vinegar that has a wonderfully sweet and sour flavor. Just like the finest olive oils, it can be very expensive. The vinegar is aged in oak casks between five and twenty years—the longer the aging process, the higher the price. It's delicious used on its own simply to dress sliced ripe tomatoes or roasted vegetable salads, or try simmering it with a little sugar to make a divine syrupy balsamic glaze for drizzling over sweet or savory salads.

SEEDS AND NUTS

A sprinkling of crunchy nuts or seeds can add plenty of extra interest to salads as well as boosting your intake of protein, essential vitamins, and minerals. Keep small quantities of pumpkin, sunflower, and sesame seeds as well as a selection of unsalted nuts in the pantry. To bring out more of their flavor, lightly toast nuts and seeds by spreading them on a baking sheet and putting under a hot broiler for a few minutes.

BEANS, PASTA, AND RICE

These great energy foods can form the basis of really substantial and filling salads. Although most have a fairly bland flavor on their own, the addition of herbs, spices, and dressings can totally transform them. Look for more unusual grains, such as quinoa, bulgur, and wild rice. For added fiber, opt for whole wheat varieties of pasta and rice.

SALAD SUCCESS

Follow these simple guidelines for the perfect salad every time!

When buying salad greens, pick ones that look fresh and crisp with no wilting or browning leaves. If you buy a prepared bag of salad greens, give the bag a good shake and check for any signs of deterioration. Only buy as much as you need because salad greens don't retain their freshness for long and, once opened, the contents of the bag will need to be consumed within 24 hours.

Store salad greens in a plastic box or unsealed bag in the salad drawer of the refrigerator. If you've bought unwashed greens from a farmers' market or grocer, don't worry about rinsing them until you are ready to use them because they will stay fresher for longer.

Bunches of cut fresh herbs with long stalks, such as parsley and mint, should be stored in the refrigerator with their stalks in a jar of water. Other herbs with shorter stems and cut basil sprigs are best kept in an open plastic bag or loosely wrapped in damp paper towels and stored in the salad drawer of the refrigerator.

To prepare salad greens, carefully separate them from the stem if necessary. Rinse in a large bowl or sink full of cold water to remove fine grit and dirt. Discard any limp, wilted, or browning leaves. Shake the excess water off the leaves, then spin until dry in a salad spinner or gently pat dry with a clean dish towel. The leaves should be thoroughly dry before tossing with a dressing, otherwise they will dilute the dressing. Salad greens can be washed and dried a few hours before serving but will need to be stored, without dressing, in the refrigerator.

Most dressings can also be prepared in advance and stored in the refrigerator. Remember they will need a thorough whisking or shaking before adding to the salad and it's also worth checking seasoning at this time as well.

Dress leafy salads just before serving and only use enough of the dressing to lightly coat the leaves, otherwise they will quickly wilt. Pour the dressing into a large, chilled serving bowl, then pile the salad loosely on top. Using salad servers or clean hands gently toss the leaves in the dressing.

If you're catering for a large number of people and serving a variety of different salads, then prepare the ones with grains, beans, or pasta first because they will keep the longest.

Side salads should complement and enhance the dishes they are served with, not overpower them, so choose carefully and only serve a small bowlful.

Timing is vital when serving warm salads. Prepare everything in advance, including the dressing. Let hot foods, such as charbroiled meats, cool slightly before completing the salad to prevent the heat from wilting salad leaves too quickly.

SALAD TECHNIQUES

PEELING TOMATOES

Choose firm ripe tomatoes for peeling. With the tip of a sharp knife, score a cross through the skin at the bottom of each tomato. Place in a heatproof bowl, cover with boiling water, and let stand for 2–3 minutes, until the skins begin to wrinkle and split. Drain and plunge the tomatoes into a bowl of ice cold water for 1–2 minutes, then drain again and peel off the skin with your fingertips.

BLANCHING VEGETABLES

This technique is used to lightly cook vegetables such as green beans and asparagus, yet still retain their crispness and color. Plunge the prepared vegetables into a pan of boiling water for about 2 minutes. Quickly drain in a colander, then refresh under cold running water to stop the cooking process.

VEGETABLE RIBBONS

These look impressive but are easy to make. Run a swivel-head vegetable peeler along the length of firm vegetables, such as carrot, cucumber, or zucchini. Use immediately or sprinkle with a little cold water, cover, and chill in the refrigerator for no longer than a couple of hours before serving.

INTRODUCTION TO OILS

Edible oil has a rich history shared by many cultures over many centuries. It is used as a cooking medium, a preservative, a medicine, and best of all—food. The Chinese and Japanese developed methods to extract oil from soy plants; Mediterranean people used olives; Mexicans and North Americans were fond of peanuts and sunflower seeds; and in Africa, palms and coconuts provided the basis for oil. Other sources of oil are cotton, safflower seeds, watermelon seeds, grape seeds, rapeseed, corn, nuts, avocados, and, of course, animals.

Thanks to the popularity of the Mediterranean diet, olive oil has captured the world's attention with its health-inducing benefits. Other beneficial oils, such as canola, are almost flavorless and present the perfect backdrop for flavorful additions.

There are just a few guidelines to follow before getting started. The most important to remember is this: Oil improperly stored can encourage the growth of bacteria. When herbs or vegetables with a high water content (such as garlic) are mixed with oil and stored in a nonrefrigerated place, an oxygen-free environment is created that can lead to botulism.

GARLIC, CHILE & OREGANO OIL

5 cloves garlic
1 red hot chile
1 tsp dried oregano
1 cup canola oil

Preheat the oven to 300°F/150°C.

Cut the garlic cloves in half lengthwise. Using gloves, remove the seeds from the chile and chop into small pieces equaling two tablespoons.

Combine the garlic, chile, and oregano with the oil in a 2-cup/500-ml glass measuring cup (make sure it is ovenproof). Place on a glass pie plate in the center of the oven and heat for 1½–2 hours. The temperature of the oil should reach 250°F/120°C if you are using a digital thermometer.

Remove from the oven, let cool, and strain through cheesecloth into a clean jar. Store covered in the refrigerator. You can also leave the garlic and chile pieces in the oil and strain before using.

PARSLEY & CILANTRO OIL

½ cup fresh flat-leaf parsley leaves
½ cup fresh cilantro leaves
1 cup canola oil

Wash and drain the leaves. Prepare a pot of water, bring to a boil, and submerge the leaves. Blanch for five seconds. Drain the leaves and dry well.

Heat the oil in a saucepan, bring to nearly boiling point, and let simmer for 1–2 minutes.

Combine the warmed oil and leaves in a blender bowl or food processor. Process until well combined. Store covered in the refrigerator.

INTRODUCTION TO VINEGARS

Our ancestors were very wise about vinegar. The ancient Babylonians used it as a preservative, the Romans drank it, Helen of Troy bathed in it, and Cleopatra dissolved a pearl in it to prove that she could consume a fortune in a single meal. It is mentioned numerous times in the Bible, and Hippocrates recommended its therapeutic properties.

As with oils, there are many types of vinegars, such as balsamic (produced from selected grapes and fermented for a long time), red and white wine vinegars, rice vinegar, and cider vinegar. There are also specialty vinegars, such as raspberry, sherry, and champagne vinegars.

Good vinegar can be utilized in so many ways. It is used to prepare and preserve food. It also has health-giving properties: A tablespoon a day of cider vinegar is said to be most beneficial. Even its hygienic properties are well-known; your grandmother was right when she told you that there is nothing like a spray of vinegar for cleaning.

Best of all, vinegar plays an important role in dressings, sauces, and mustards. It adds just the right kick to a barbecue sauce; it brings tanginess to a vinaigrette; it sweetens a wine reduction sauce. Infusing vinegar with other flavors is a great way to add yet another layer of aroma and flavor.

BASIL, CHIVE & LEMON VINEGAR

zest of ½ lemon

5 basil leaves

10 stalks chives

1 cup white wine vinegar

When peeling the lemon for the zest (using only half the lemon), be sure to avoid the white pith. Wash and dry the basil leaves and the chives, then crush them or chop coarsely. Place the zest, basil, and chives in a clean jar.

In a saucepan over medium heat, heat the white wine vinegar until it starts to bubble around the edges of the pan. Wait until it cools just a little, then add it to the jar with the other ingredients. When it is completely cool, cover the jar and store in a cool, dark, and dry place.

ROSEMARY & GARLIC BALSAMIC VINEGAR

ten 2-inch/5-cm sprigs rosemary

4 cloves garlic

1 cup balsamic vinegar

Wash the rosemary sprigs, dry, and tear off the leaves from the stems. Split the garlic cloves in half lengthwise. Combine the leaves and garlic halves in a clean jar.

In a saucepan over medium heat, heat the balsamic vinegar until it just starts to bubble around the edges of the pan. Wait until it cools a little, then pour into the jar with the rosemary and garlic. When it is completely cool, cover the jar and store in a cool, dark place. Check occasionally to see whether the vinegar has reached the desired strength.

Before using, strain the vinegar through a fine sieve or cheesecloth into clean jars. Add a fresh sprig of rosemary for decoration, cover again, and store in a cool, dark place.

MEAT

WARM BEEF
SALAD NIÇOISE

Place the steaks in a shallow dish. Blend the vinegar with
1 tablespoon of orange juice and 1 teaspoon of mustard. Pour
over the steaks, cover, then let stand in the refrigerator for at
least 30 minutes. Turn over halfway through the marinating time.

Place the eggs in a pan and cover with cold water. Bring to a
boil, then reduce the heat to a simmer and cook for 10 minutes.
Remove and plunge the eggs into cold water. Once cold, shell
and set aside.

Meanwhile, place the potatoes in a pan and cover with cold
water. Bring to a boil, then cover and let simmer for 15 minutes,
or until tender when pierced with a fork. Drain and set aside.

Bring a saucepan of water to a boil, add the beans and cook for
5 minutes, or until just tender. Drain, plunge into cold water, and
drain again. Arrange the potatoes and beans on top of the salad
leaves together with the bell pepper, cherry tomatoes, and olives,
if using. Blend the remaining orange juice and mustard with the
olive oil and set aside.

Heat a stove-top grill pan or griddle until smoking. Drain the
steaks and cook for 3–5 minutes on each side or according to
personal preference. Slice the steaks and arrange on top of the
salad, then pour over the dressing and serve.

SERVES 4

4 tenderloin steaks,
   about 4 oz/115 g each,
   trimmed of any visible fat

2 tbsp red wine vinegar

2 tbsp orange juice

2 tsp prepared English mustard

2 eggs

6 oz/175 g new potatoes

¾ cup trimmed green beans

4–6 cups mixed salad greens,
   such as baby spinach, arugula,
   and mizuna

1 yellow bell pepper, seeded,
   peeled, and cut into strips

12 cherry tomatoes, halved

black olives, pitted (optional)

2 tsp extra virgin olive oil

ROAST BEEF SALAD

Preheat the oven to 425°F/220°C. Rub the beef with pepper to taste and Worcestershire sauce. Heat 2 tablespoons of the oil in a small roasting pan over high heat, add the beef, and sear on all sides. Transfer the dish to the preheated oven and roast for 30 minutes. Remove and let cool. Cut into thin slices.

Bring a large pan of water to a boil, add the beans, and cook for 5 minutes, or until just tender. Remove with a slotted spoon and refresh the beans under cold running water. Drain and put into a large bowl.

Return the beans' cooking water to a boil, add the pasta, and cook for 12 minutes, or until tender. Drain, return to the pan, and toss with the remaining oil.

Add the pasta to the beans with the onions, radicchio leaves, olives, and hazelnuts, mix gently, and transfer to a serving bowl or dish. Arrange some thinly sliced beef on top.

Whisk the dressing ingredients together in a separate bowl, then pour over the salad and serve at once with extra sliced beef.

SERVES 4

1 lb 10 oz/750 g beef tenderloin, trimmed of any visible fat

2 tsp Worcestershire sauce

3 tbsp olive oil

14 oz/400 g green beans, trimmed and halved

3½ oz/100 g small pasta shapes, such as orecchiette

2 red onions, finely sliced

1 large head radicchio

generous ¼ cup green olives, pitted

scant ⅓ cup shelled hazelnuts, whole

pepper

dressing

1 tsp Dijon mustard

2 tbsp white wine vinegar

5 tbsp olive oil

BEEF SATAY SALAD

SERVES 4

2 sirloin steaks, each weighing
   about 8 oz/225 g

2 tbsp soy sauce

1 tbsp lime juice

1 garlic clove, crushed

1 tsp dried chili flakes

3¾ cups shredded Chinese
   cabbage

¼ cucumber, thinly sliced

4 scallions, sliced

fresh cilantro leaves and sliced
   red chile, to garnish

lime wedges, to serve

satay dressing

2 tbsp crunchy peanut butter

3 tbsp coconut milk

1 tbsp soy sauce

1 tbsp lime juice

2 tsp soft brown sugar

Put the steaks into a shallow dish. Combine the soy sauce, lime juice, garlic, and chili flakes and pour the mixture over the steaks. Cover and let marinate at room temperature for 1 hour.

Heat a cast-iron grill pan until very hot. Add the steaks and cook for 3–5 minutes on each side, depending on how well done you like your steak. Transfer the steaks to a plate, cover, and let rest for 5 minutes.

To make the dressing, put all the ingredients into a small pan and heat gently, stirring constantly, until the peanut butter has melted. Simmer for 1 minute. If the dressing becomes too thick, add a little water and stir well to make a pouring consistency.

Combine the Chinese cabbage, cucumber, and scallions and put them on a serving platter. Thinly slice the steaks and arrange them on top of the salad. Drizzle the satay dressing over them and garnish with cilantro leaves and chile slices. Serve with lime wedges.

SICHUAN NUMBING BEEF SALAD

Slice the beef into ½ x 1½ inches/1 x 4 cm pieces. Combine the marinade ingredients and pour over the beef. Marinate at room temperature for 30 minutes, or in the refrigerator for up to 2 days.

Cook the noodles according to the package directions and let cool. Snip into shorter lengths. Whisk the dressing ingredients together in a separate bowl. Combine the noodles, onion, radishes, and peppery leaves in a large bowl. Whisk the dressing again and pour two-thirds of it over the salad. Toss to distribute the noodles, then divide between individual serving plates.

Heat a wok over medium–high heat, then add the peanut oil and Sichuan pepper. Stir for a few seconds to flavor the oil. Add the beef and marinade and stir-fry for 4–5 minutes, until caramelized. Remove with a slotted spoon and scatter over the salad. Pour over the remaining dressing.

SERVES 4

12 oz/350 g porterhouse steak, trimmed of any visible fat

3½ oz/90 g egg noodles

1 small red onion, halved and thinly sliced

6 radishes, sliced

4 good handfuls peppery leaves, such as tatsoi, mustard greens, and arugula

1½ tbsp peanut oil

1 tsp Sichuan pepper, crushed

marinade

4 tsp Chinese rice wine or dry sherry

½ tbsp soy sauce

4 tsp sugar

2 tbsp hoisin sauce

1-inch/2.5-cm piece fresh ginger, squeezed in a garlic press

dressing

2 tsp Sichuan pepper, crushed

1½ tbsp light soy sauce

1½ tbsp rice vinegar

2 tbsp cold-pressed sesame oil

STEAK WALDORF SALAD

Heat a cast-iron grill pan or heavy-bottom skillet over medium heat. Brush each steak with oil and season to taste with pepper. Add the steaks to the pan and cook for 6–7 minutes for rare or 8–10 minutes for medium, turning the steaks frequently and brushing once or twice with oil. Remove from the pan and set aside.

Meanwhile, stir the mustard into the mayonnaise. Put the lemon juice into a large bowl. Peel and core the apples, then cut them into small chunks and immediately toss in the lemon juice. Stir in the mustard mayonnaise. Add the celery and walnuts to the apple mixture and toss together.

Arrange the salad greens on 4 plates, then divide the apple mixture among them. Very thinly slice the steaks, arrange on top of the salads, and serve immediately with bread.

SERVES 4

2 tenderloin steaks,
   about 6 oz/175 g each
   and 1 inch/2.5 cm thick

olive or corn oil, for brushing

1 tbsp whole-grain mustard

²⁄₃ cup mayonnaise

1 tbsp lemon juice

1 lb 2 oz/500 g apples

4 celery stalks, thinly sliced

½ cup walnut halves,
   broken into pieces

4 cups mixed salad greens

pepper

fresh whole wheat bread, to serve

WARM BACON & EGG SALAD

SERVES 4

2 romaine lettuce hearts,
   coarsely torn

4 eggs

2 tbsp sunflower oil

2 thick slices of bread, crusts
   removed and cubed

1⅓ cups cubed smoked bacon

12 cherry tomatoes, halved

dressing

2 tbsp extra virgin olive oil

1 tbsp red wine vinegar

1 tsp Dijon mustard

pepper

To make the dressing, whisk the dressing ingredients together in a bowl. Put the lettuce leaves into a salad bowl.

Put the eggs into a pan and cover with cold water. Bring to a boil and boil for 4 minutes. Drain and plunge the eggs into cold water for 2 minutes. Peel off the shells and cut into quarters.

Heat the sunflower oil in a large skillet and fry the bread cubes, turning frequently, for 3–4 minutes, until golden brown. Remove with a slotted spoon and set aside.

Add the bacon to the skillet and cook over medium–high heat, until crisp and golden. Add the tomatoes and dressing to the skillet and cook for another minute.

Gently toss the bacon, tomatoes, and dressing into the lettuce leaves. Add the quartered eggs and sprinkle with the croutons. Serve immediately.

MEAT

BLT SALAD

Preheat the broiler to high. Put the bacon slices on the broiler pan and broil for 3–4 minutes, turning once, until crisp.

To make the dressing, whisk the dressing ingredients together in a bowl.

Divide the lettuce wedges among 4 serving plates with the tomatoes and cucumber. Toss the avocado slices in the lemon juice and add to the salads.

Drizzle the dressing over the salads. Halve the bacon slices and stack them on top of the salads. Sprinkle the grated cheese over them, if using, and serve immediately.

SERVES 4

8 thick slices lean bacon

1 iceberg lettuce, cut into 12 wedges

2 beefsteak tomatoes, sliced into wedges

¼ cucumber, thickly sliced

½ ripe avocado, peeled, pitted, and sliced

1 tbsp lemon juice

¾ cup coarsely grated cheddar cheese (optional)

dressing

4 tbsp mayonnaise

2 tbsp sour cream

1 tbsp milk

2 tsp whole-grain mustard

salt and pepper

CRISPY SPINACH & BACON SALAD

Heat 2 tablespoons of the olive oil over high heat in a large skillet. Add the diced bacon to the skillet and cook for 3–4 minutes, or until crisp. Remove with a slotted spoon, draining carefully, and set aside.

Toss the cubes of bread in the fat remaining in the skillet over high heat for about 4 minutes, or until crisp and golden. Remove the croutons with a slotted spoon, draining carefully, and set them aside.

Add the remaining oil to the skillet and heat. Toss the spinach in the oil over high heat for about 3 minutes, or until it has just wilted. Turn into a serving bowl and sprinkle with the bacon and croutons. Serve immediately.

SERVES 4

4 tbsp olive oil

4 slices lean bacon, diced

1 slice thick white bread, crusts removed, cut into cubes

1 lb/450 g fresh spinach, torn or shredded

WALNUT, PEAR & CRISPY BACON SALAD

SERVES 4

4 slices lean bacon

scant ¾ cup walnut halves

2 Red Bartlett pears, cored and
   sliced lengthwise

1 tbsp lemon juice

2 bunches watercress,
   tough stalks removed

dressing

3 tbsp extra virgin olive oil

2 tbsp lemon juice

½ tsp honey

salt and pepper

Preheat the broiler to high. Put the bacon slices on the broiler pan and broil for 3–4 minutes, turning once, until crisp. Let cool, then cut into ½-inch/1-cm pieces.

Meanwhile, heat a dry skillet over medium heat and lightly toast the walnuts, shaking the skillet frequently, for 3 minutes, or until lightly browned. Let cool.

Toss the pears in the lemon juice to prevent discoloration. Put the watercress, walnuts, pears, and bacon into a salad bowl.

To make the dressing, whisk the dressing ingredients together in a separate bowl. Pour over the salad, toss well to combine, and serve.

ROAST PORK & PUMPKIN SALAD

Preheat the oven to 400°F/200°C. Cut the pumpkin in half, scoop out the seeds and fibers, and cut the flesh into wedges about 1½ inches/4 cm wide. Very lightly brush the pumpkin and onion wedges with the olive oil, place in a roasting pan, and roast for 25–30 minutes, until the pumpkin and onions are tender but holding their shape.

Meanwhile, bring a small pan of salted water to a boil. Add the green beans and blanch for 5 minutes, or until tender. Drain well and cool under cold running water to stop them from cooking further. Drain well and pat dry.

Remove the pumpkin and onion wedges from the oven as soon as they are tender-crisp and let cool completely. When the pumpkin is cool, peel and cut into bite-size pieces.

To make the vinaigrette, place all the ingredients in a screw-top jar and shake vigorously until they are well blended.

To assemble the salad, put the pumpkins, onions, beans, pork, arugula, feta, pine nuts, and parsley in a large bowl and gently toss together—be careful not to break up the pumpkin. Shake the dressing again, pour over the salad, and gently toss. Divide among individual bowls and serve.

SERVES 4–6

1 small pumpkin, about
  3½ lb/1.6 kg

2 red onions, cut into wedges

olive oil, for brushing

¾ cup trimmed and halved green
  beans

1¼ lb/600 g roast pork, any skin
  or rind removed and cut into
  bite-size chunks

large handful fresh arugula leaves

3½ oz/100 g feta cheese, drained
  and crumbled

2 tbsp toasted pine nuts

2 tbsp chopped fresh flat-leaf
  parsley

salt and pepper

vinaigrette

6 tbsp extra virgin olive oil

3 tbsp balsamic vinegar

½ tsp sugar

½ tsp Dijon, prepared English,
  or whole-grain mustard

HOISIN PORK WITH RIBBON SALAD

Cut the pork tenderloin into 2 pieces and put them into a shallow dish. Pour the hoisin sauce over them, cover, and let marinate at room temperature for 1 hour.

Preheat the oven to 375°F/ 190°C.

Put the pork on a wire rack set over a roasting pan filled halfway with water (this helps to keep the pork moist during cooking). Roast for 35–40 minutes, until the pork is cooked through and lightly charred in places. Let cool for 10 minutes.

To make the ribbon salad, use a vegetable peeler to slice the carrots and cucumber into thin ribbons. Put them into a bowl and toss together with the scallions and radishes.

Heat a nonstick skillet and add the sesame seeds. Cook over medium heat for 3–4 minutes, until lightly toasted. Add to the salad. Whisk together the sesame oil and vinegar and pour half the dressing over the salad. Toss well to mix.

Slice the pork tenderloin and transfer to individual serving plates with the ribbon salad on the side. Drizzle the rest of the dressing over the pork and serve immediately.

SERVES 4

1 lb/450 g pork tenderloin

3 tbsp hoisin sauce

2 tbsp sesame seeds

ribbon salad

3 medium carrots

½ cucumber

4 scallions, finely shredded

4 radishes, very thinly sliced

dressing

2 tbsp toasted sesame oil

2 tbsp rice vinegar

PORK & CUCUMBER SALAD

SERVES 4

1 lb/450 g pork tenderloin, trimmed of any visible fat

6 scallions, halved lengthwise and sliced into 3

1 cucumber

4 handfuls shredded iceberg lettuce

1 cup cilantro leaves

½ cup mint leaves

4 tbsp lightly crushed dry-roast peanuts

finely grated zest of 1 lime

1 tsp salt

1 tsp sugar

1 tbsp kechap manis, or dark soy sauce

1 tbsp peanut oil

2 tsp sesame oil

marinade

2 small fresh red chiles, seeded and finely chopped

4 tbsp sugar

3 tbsp Thai fish sauce

4 tbsp lime juice

4 tbsp rice vinegar

Thinly slice the pork. Cut each slice in half lengthwise. Put in a bowl with the scallions.

Peel the cucumber, halve lengthwise, and scoop out the seeds. Thinly slice diagonally and put in a bowl.

Next make the marinade. Using a large mortar and pestle, pound the chopped chiles and the sugar to a watery, red paste. Add the Thai fish sauce, lime juice, and rice vinegar, stirring to dissolve the sugar. Pour into a pitcher. Pour one-half over the pork and scallions and one-half over the cucumber. Marinate for 1 hour, then drain the cucumber and reserve its marinade.

Put the shredded lettuce, cilantro, and mint in a bowl and toss to mix. Divide between individual serving plates. Arrange the cucumber slices on top and dress with the reserved marinade.

Mix the nuts with the lime zest, salt, and sugar.

Drain the pork and discard the marinade. Toss the pork with the kechap manis. Heat a wok over high heat, then add the oils. Stir-fry the pork for 5 minutes, until cooked through and slightly caramelized. Arrange the pork slices on top of the cucumber and sprinkle with the nut mixture. Serve at once.

SPINACH & PANCETTA SALAD

To make the dressing, whisk the dressing ingredients together in a bowl. Rinse the baby spinach under cold running water, then drain and place in a large salad bowl.

Heat the oil in a large skillet. Add the pancetta and cook for 3 minutes. Add the mushrooms and cook for 3–4 minutes, or until tender.

Pour the dressing into the skillet and immediately turn the cooked mixture and dressing into the bowl with the spinach. Toss until coated with the dressing and serve at once.

SERVES 4

generous 6 cups fresh baby spinach leaves

2 tbsp olive oil

5½ oz/150 g pancetta

10 oz/280 g mixed wild mushrooms, sliced

dressing

5 tbsp olive oil

1 tbsp balsamic vinegar

1 tsp Dijon mustard

pinch of sugar

salt and pepper

PASTRAMI & BELL PEPPER ANTIPASTI SALAD

Tear the lettuce into small chunks and put them into a serving bowl. Drain the bell pepper antipasto and sun-blush tomatoes, reserving 4 tablespoons of the oil. Coarsely chop the bell peppers and tomatoes and toss into the lettuce with the olives.

To make the dressing, combine the reserved oil, the vinegar, mustard, and sugar in a separate bowl and season to taste with salt and pepper. Pour half the dressing over the salad and toss well to mix. Arrange the pastrami in ruffles on top of the salad. Serve drizzled with the rest of the dressing and garnished with basil leaves.

SERVES 4

1 iceberg lettuce

10 oz/280 g charbroiled bell pepper antipasto in oil

1 cup sun-blush tomatoes or sun-dried tomatoes in oil

1 cup pitted green olives

4 oz/115 g wafer-thin pastrami slices

fresh basil leaves, to garnish

dressing

2 tbsp balsamic vinegar

1 tsp Dijon mustard

pinch of sugar

salt and pepper

ARTICHOKE & PROSCIUTTO SALAD

SERVES 4

9¾ oz/275 g canned artichoke hearts in oil, drained

4 small tomatoes

¼ cup sun-dried tomatoes in oil, drained

1½ oz/40 g prosciutto

1 tbsp pitted and halved black olives

handful of fresh basil sprigs

fresh crusty bread, to serve

dressing

3 tbsp olive oil

1 tbsp white wine vinegar

1 garlic clove, crushed

½ tsp mild mustard

1 tsp honey

salt and pepper

Make sure the artichoke hearts are thoroughly drained, then cut them into quarters and place in a serving bowl. Cut each tomato into wedges. Slice the sun-dried tomatoes into thin strips. Cut the prosciutto into thin strips and add to the bowl with the tomatoes and olive halves.

Keeping a few basil sprigs whole for garnishing, tear the remainder of the leaves into small pieces and add to the bowl containing the other salad ingredients.

To make the dressing, place all the ingredients in a screw-top jar and shake vigorously until they are well blended.

Pour the dressing over the salad and toss together. Garnish the salad with a few basil sprigs and serve with crusty bread.

HAM & SALAMI SALAD WITH FIGS

Trim the stems of the figs to leave just a short length, then cut the figs into quarters.

Arrange the ham and salami on a large serving platter.

Wash and dry the herbs and arugula and put in a bowl with the prepared figs.

To make the dressing, whisk the lemon juice and oil together in a separate bowl and season well with salt and pepper. Pour over the herbs and salad greens and carefully turn the figs and greens in the dressing until they are well coated.

Spoon the figs and salad onto the meat and arrange around the platter.

SERVES 6

9–12 ripe figs, depending on size

6 thin slices dry-cured Italian ham

12 thin slices salami

1 small bunch fresh basil, separated into small sprigs

few fresh mint sprigs

1 small bunch arugula leaves

dressing

2 tbsp freshly squeezed lemon juice

4 tbsp extra virgin olive oil

salt and pepper

SALAMI PASTA SALAD

Bring a large pan of lightly salted water to a boil. Add the pasta and return to a boil. Cook for 10–12 minutes, until just tender, or cook according to the package directions.

Drain the pasta well and transfer to a bowl. Combine the pesto sauce and olive oil and stir the mixture into the hot pasta. Let cool, stirring occasionally.

Add the bell peppers, onion, olives, tomatoes, salami, and mozzarella cheese to the pasta and toss well to mix. Season to taste with salt and pepper. Serve garnished with the basil sprigs.

SERVES 4–6

12 oz/350 g dried pasta tubes, such as penne

2 tbsp pesto sauce

3 tbsp olive oil

1 orange bell pepper, seeded and diced

1 yellow bell pepper, seeded and diced

1 red onion, finely diced

¾ cup pitted black olives

6 cherry tomatoes, halved

6-oz/175-g piece Milano salami, cut into small chunks

4½ oz/125 g mozzarella cheese, torn into small pieces

salt and pepper

fresh basil sprigs, to garnish

ONION & HERB SALAD WITH SPICY SAUSAGE

SERVES 2

1 tbsp corn oil

1 small onion, finely sliced

9 oz/250 g canned lima beans, drained and rinsed

1 tsp balsamic vinegar

2 spicy sausages, sliced diagonally

1 small tomato, diced

2 tbsp harissa paste

3 cups mixed herb salad

Heat the oil in a nonstick skillet over medium heat, add the onion, and cook, stirring frequently, until softened but not browned. Add the beans and cook for an additional 1 minute, then add the vinegar, stirring well. Keep warm.

Meanwhile, heat a separate dry skillet over medium heat, add the sausage slices, and cook, turning occasionally, until lightly browned. Remove with a slotted spoon and drain on paper towels.

Mix the tomato and harissa paste together in a small bowl. Divide the herb salad between 2 plates, spoon over the bean mixture, and sprinkle over the warm sausage slices. Top with a spoonful of the tomato-and-harissa mixture and serve at once.

SPICY SAUSAGE
PASTA SALAD

Bring a large pan of lightly salted water to a boil. Add the pasta and return to a boil. Cook for 8–10 minutes, until just tender, or cook according to the package directions. Drain and set aside.

Heat the oil in a pan over medium heat. Add the onion and cook until translucent, then stir in the garlic, yellow bell pepper, and sausage and cook for 3–4 minutes, stirring once or twice.

Add the wine, vinegar, and reserved pasta to the pan, stir, and bring the mixture just to a boil over medium heat.

Arrange the salad greens on serving plates, spoon over the warm sausage-and-pasta mixture, and serve immediately.

SERVES 4

4½ oz/125 g dried pasta shells, such as conchiglie

2 tbsp olive oil

1 medium onion, chopped

2 garlic cloves, finely chopped

1 small yellow bell pepper, seeded and cut into thin strips

6 oz/175 g spicy pork sausage, such as chorizo, pepperoni, or salami, skinned and sliced

2 tbsp red wine

1 tbsp red wine vinegar

4 cups mixed salad greens

salt

HOT SAUSAGE & POTATO SALAD

Bring a large pan of lightly salted water to a boil. Add the potatoes and cook for 12–15 minutes, or until just tender.

Meanwhile, heat the sunflower oil in a large skillet and cook the sausages for 5 minutes. Add the onions to the skillet and continue cooking, turning frequently, for another 8–10 minutes, until the sausages are cooked through and the onions are golden and tender. Remove the onions and sausages from the skillet and drain on paper towels. Slice each sausage diagonally into 4 pieces.

Drain the potatoes and put them into a large bowl with the onions and sausages.

To make the dressing, place all the ingredients in a screw-top jar and shake vigorously until they are well blended. Pour the dressing over the hot salad and toss well to coat. Adjust the seasoning to taste. Serve immediately.

SERVES 4

1 lb 9 oz/700 g new potatoes, halved

1 tbsp sunflower oil

6 thick pork sausages

2 onions, sliced into thin wedges

dressing

4 tbsp olive oil

1 tbsp white wine vinegar

2 tsp whole-grain mustard

2 tsp honey

salt and pepper

ARTICHOKE & SPICY SAUSAGE SALAD

SERVES 8

12 small globe artichokes

juice of ½ lemon

2 tbsp Spanish olive oil

1 small orange-fleshed melon,
  such as cantaloupe

7 oz/200 g cooked spicy sausage,
  outer casing removed

fresh tarragon or flat-leaf parsley
  sprigs, to garnish

dressing

3 tbsp extra virgin olive oil

1 tbsp red wine vinegar

1 tsp prepared mustard

1 tbsp chopped fresh tarragon

salt and pepper

Prepare the artichokes, then brush the cut surfaces of the artichokes with lemon juice to prevent discoloration. Carefully remove the choke (the mass of silky hairs) by pulling it out with your fingers or by scooping it out with a spoon. It is very important to remove all the choke on older artichokes, because the little barbs, if eaten, can irritate the throat. Cut the artichokes into fourths and brush them again with lemon juice.

Heat the olive oil in a large, heavy-bottom skillet. Add the prepared artichokes and cook, stirring frequently, for 5 minutes, or until the artichoke leaves are golden brown. Remove from the skillet, then transfer to a large serving bowl and let cool.

To prepare the melon, cut in half and scoop out the seeds with a spoon. Cut the flesh into bite-size cubes. Add to the cooled artichokes. Cut the sausage into bite-size chunks and add to the melon and artichokes.

To make the dressing, whisk the dressing ingredients together in a separate bowl. Just before serving, pour the dressing over the prepared salad ingredients and toss together. Serve the salad garnished with tarragon.

BROILED LAMB WITH YOGURT DRESSING

Mix the oil, tomato paste, cumin, lemon juice, garlic, cayenne, and salt and pepper to taste together in a nonmetallic bowl. Add the lamb and rub all over with the marinade. Cover the bowl and marinate in the refrigerator for at least 2 hours, but ideally overnight.

Meanwhile, to make the dressing, whisk the lemon juice and honey together until the honey dissolves. Whisk in the yogurt until well blended. Stir in the herbs and add salt and pepper to taste. Cover and chill until required.

Remove the lamb from the refrigerator 15 minutes before you are ready to cook. Heat the broiler to its highest setting and lightly brush the broiler rack with oil. Broil the lamb, turning it once, for 10 minutes for medium and 12 minutes for well done. Let the lamb cool completely, then cover and chill until required.

Thinly slice the lamb, then divide among 4 plates. Adjust the seasoning in the dressing, if necessary, then spoon over the lamb slices. Sprinkle with toasted sesame seeds and parsley and serve.

SERVES 4

2 tbsp sunflower oil, plus extra for brushing

1 tbsp tomato paste

½ tbsp ground cumin

1 tsp lemon juice

1 garlic clove, crushed

pinch of cayenne pepper

1 lb 2 oz/500 g lamb neck fillets, trimmed of any visible fat

salt and pepper

toasted sesame seeds and chopped fresh flat-leaf parsley, to garnish

dressing

2 tbsp fresh lemon juice

1 tsp honey

⅓ cup thick plain yogurt

2 tbsp finely shredded fresh mint

2 tbsp chopped fresh parsley

1 tbsp finely snipped fresh chives

LAMB KOFTE & HERB SALAD

Put 8 wooden skewers into a shallow bowl of cold water and let soak for 30 minutes. Put the lamb, onion, spices, cilantro, and mint into a food processor with plenty of salt and pepper. Process for 1–2 minutes, until finely ground. Transfer to a bowl, cover, and chill in the refrigerator for 30 minutes.

Preheat the broiler to high. Divide the mixture into 8. Wrap the mixture around the soaked wooden skewers to form oval shapes. Brush with a little of the oil and broil under the broiler, turning frequently, for 15–20 minutes, until cooked through.

Meanwhile, combine the yogurt, cucumber, and mint sauce in a small bowl and season with salt and pepper.

Put the salad greens into a large bowl. Whisk the rest of the oil with the lemon juice and season to taste. Pour the dressing over the salad greens and toss to coat. Serve the hot koftes, on or off the skewers, with the salad and cucumber-and-mint yogurt.

SERVES 4

1³⁄₄ cups lean ground lamb

1 small onion, finely chopped

2 tsp each ground coriander, ground cumin, and paprika

1 tbsp chopped fresh cilantro

2 tbsp chopped fresh mint

3 tbsp olive oil

6 tbsp plain yogurt

2¹⁄₂–inch-/5-cm piece cucumber, grated

2 tsp mint sauce

4 cups mixed baby leaf and herb salad

1 tbsp lemon juice

salt and pepper

POULTRY

LAYERED
CHICKEN SALAD

Preheat the broiler to high. Put the potatoes into a large pan, add just enough cold water to cover, and bring to a boil. Lower the heat, cover, and simmer for 15–20 minutes, until tender. Meanwhile, place the bell pepper halves, skin side up, under the preheated broiler and broil until the skins blacken and begin to char.

Remove the bell peppers with tongs, place in a bowl, and cover with plastic wrap. Set aside until cool enough to handle, then peel off the skins and slice the flesh.

Bring a small pan of lightly salted water to a boil. Add the zucchini, bring back to a boil, and simmer for 3 minutes. Drain, rinse under cold running water to prevent any further cooking, and drain again. Set aside.

To make the dressing, whisk the dressing ingredients together in a separate bowl.

When the potatoes are tender, drain, cool, and slice them. Add them to the dressing and mix gently to coat evenly. Spoon the potatoes onto 4 serving plates, dividing them equally.

Top each plate with one-quarter of the bell pepper slices and zucchini. Layer one-quarter of the onion and tomato slices, then the sliced chicken, on top of each serving. Garnish with chopped chives and serve immediately.

SERVES 4

1 lb 10 oz/750 g new potatoes, scrubbed

1 red bell pepper, halved and seeded

1 green bell pepper, halved and seeded

2 small zucchini, sliced

1 small onion, thinly sliced

3 tomatoes, sliced

12 oz/350 g cooked boneless chicken, sliced

chopped fresh chives, to garnish

dressing

$^2/_3$ cup plain yogurt

3 tbsp mayonnaise

1 tbsp chopped fresh chives

salt and pepper

CORONATION
CHICKEN SALAD

Heat the oil in a skillet. Add the cashew nuts and almonds and cook for 2–3 minutes, until golden. Remove with a slotted spoon and drain on paper towels.

Add the onion to the skillet and cook gently for 6–7 minutes, until softened and golden. Stir in the curry paste and cook for another minute. Transfer to a bowl and let cool.

Stir the mayonnaise, yogurt, and mango chutney into the onion and mix well. Tear the chicken into large strips and add to the dressing. Toss well to coat. Season with salt and pepper.

Put the salad greens into a shallow serving bowl. Add the curried chicken and mango slices to the bowl and toss gently into the salad greens. Sprinkle the nuts over the salad and serve garnished with cilantro leaves.

SERVES 4

1 tbsp sunflower oil

1 tbsp unsalted cashew nuts

1 tbsp whole blanched almonds

1 onion, chopped

1 tbsp mild curry paste

4 tbsp mayonnaise

4 tbsp plain yogurt

1 tbsp mango chutney

1 lb/450 g cooked skinless, boneless chicken, sliced

5 cups watercress, spinach, and arugula salad

1 small mango, peeled, pitted, and sliced

salt and pepper

fresh cilantro leaves, to garnish

CHICKEN & CHEESE SALAD

SERVES 4

5½ oz/150 g arugula leaves

2 celery stalks, trimmed and sliced

½ cucumber, sliced

2 scallions, trimmed and sliced

2 tbsp chopped fresh flat-leaf
   parsley

¼ cup walnut pieces

12 oz/350 g cooked boneless
   chicken, sliced

4½ oz/125 g bleu cheese, cubed

handful of seedless red grapes,
   cut in half (optional)

salt and pepper

dressing

2 tbsp olive oil

1 tbsp sherry vinegar

1 tsp Dijon mustard

1 tbsp chopped mixed herbs

Wash the arugula leaves, pat dry with paper towels, and put them into a large salad bowl. Add the celery, cucumber, scallions, parsley, and walnuts and mix together well. Transfer onto a large serving platter. Arrange the chicken slices over the salad, then scatter over the cheese. Add the red grapes, if using. Season well with salt and pepper.

To make the dressing, whisk the dressing ingredients together in a separate bowl. Drizzle the dressing over the salad and serve.

SMOKED
CHICKEN SALAD

To make the dressing, put the avocado, lemon juice, and vinegar in a blender or food processor and blend until smooth, scraping down the side with a rubber spatula. Add the yogurt, garlic, and tarragon leaves and process again. Season with salt and pepper to taste, then transfer to a bowl. Cover closely with plastic wrap and chill for 2 hours.

To assemble the salad, divide the tomato slices among 4–6 individual plates. Toss the smoked chicken, watercress, bean sprouts, and parsley together. Divide the salad ingredients among the plates.

Adjust the seasoning in the dressing, if necessary. Spoon the dressing over each salad and serve.

SERVES 4–6

2 large, juicy tomatoes, sliced

1 lb 5 oz/600 g cooked, smoked chicken, skinned and cut into slices

3 bunches fresh watercress, any thick stems or yellow leaves removed, then rinsed and patted dry

¾ cup fresh bean sprouts, soaked for 20 minutes in cold water, then drained well and patted dry

leaves from several sprigs fresh flat-leaf parsley or cilantro

dressing

1 ripe, soft avocado

2 tbsp lemon juice

1 tbsp tarragon vinegar

⅓ cup thick plain yogurt

1 small garlic clove, crushed

1 tbsp chopped fresh tarragon leaves

salt and pepper

CHICKEN AVOCADO SALAD

To make the dressing, place all the ingredients in a screw-top jar and shake vigorously until they are well blended.

Put the salad greens into a bowl, add about one-third of the dressing, and lightly toss. Add the chicken, satsumas, celery, onion, chives, and the remaining dressing and toss again.

Cut the avocados in half and remove the pit, then peel away the skin. Cut the flesh into thin slices, add to the other ingredients, and gently toss together, making sure the avocado slices are completely coated with dressing so they don't discolor.

Arrange on individual plates, sprinkle with sunflower seeds, and serve with pita chips on the side.

SERVES 4

4 large handfuls mixed salad greens, such as beet greens, escarole, endive, and radicchio

14 oz/400 g cooked skinless, boneless chicken, cut into bite-size pieces

2 satsumas, separated into segments

2 celery stalks, thinly sliced

½ red onion, halved and thinly sliced

2 tbsp snipped fresh chives

2 avocados

2 tbsp toasted sunflower seeds, to garnish

pita chips, to serve

dressing

½ cup extra virgin olive oil

3 tbsp Chinese rice wine vinegar

½ tsp Dijon mustard

salt and pepper

ROAST CHICKEN WITH PESTO CREAM SALAD

SERVES 4–6

1 lb 5 oz/600 g cooked skinless, boneless chicken, cut into bite-size chunks

3 celery stalks, chopped

2 large, skinned red bell peppers from a jar, well drained and sliced

salt and pepper

iceberg lettuce leaves, to serve

pesto cream

²/₃ cup sour cream

about 4 tbsp prepared pesto sauce

To make the pesto cream, put the sour cream into a large bowl, then beat in 4 tablespoons of the pesto sauce. Taste and add more pesto if you want a stronger flavor.

Add the chicken, celery, and bell peppers to the bowl and gently toss together. Add salt and pepper to taste and toss again. Cover and chill until required.

Remove the salad from the refrigerator 10 minutes before serving to return to room temperature. Give the salad ingredients a good stir, then divide among individual plates lined with lettuce leaves.

CHICKEN & PANCETTA CAESAR SALAD

To make the dressing, put all the ingredients into a food processor and process until smooth.

Heat a large nonstick skillet and add the pancetta slices. Cook over high heat for about 2 minutes, until crisp. Remove with a slotted spoon and drain on paper towels. Add the chicken to the skillet and cook over medium–high heat for 5–6 minutes, until golden and cooked through. Remove and drain with the pancetta.

Add the garlic and oil to the skillet and stir in the bread cubes. Cook over high heat, turning frequently, for 2–3 minutes, until crisp and golden.

Put the lettuce and dressing into a serving bowl and toss together thoroughly. Add the pancetta and chicken and toss in gently. Sprinkle with the garlic croutons and Parmesan cheese shavings and serve immediately.

SERVES 2

12 thin slices smoked pancetta

8 oz/225 g skinless, boneless chicken breasts, cubed

1 garlic clove, crushed

3 tbsp olive oil

1 small rustic or ciabatta roll, cut into chunky cubes

1 small romaine lettuce, chopped into large pieces

fresh Parmesan cheese shavings, to serve

dressing

3 tbsp mayonnaise

2 tbsp sour cream

1 tbsp milk

1 small garlic clove, crushed

½ tsp Dijon mustard

2 tbsp finely grated Parmesan cheese

2 anchovy fillets in oil, drained and finely chopped

pepper

WARM CHICKEN LIVER SALAD

Arrange the salad greens on serving plates.

Heat the oil in a nonstick skillet, add the onion, and cook for 5 minutes, or until softened. Add the chicken livers, tarragon, and mustard and cook for 3–5 minutes, stirring, until tender. Put on top of the salad greens.

Add the vinegar, salt, and pepper to the skillet and heat, stirring constantly, until all the sediment has been lifted from the skillet. Pour the dressing over the chicken livers and serve warm.

SERVES 4

8 oz/225 g package salad greens

1 tbsp olive oil

1 small onion, chopped finely

1 lb/450 g frozen chicken livers, thawed

1 tsp chopped fresh tarragon

1 tsp whole-grain mustard

2 tbsp balsamic vinegar

salt and pepper

CHINESE CHICKEN SALAD

SERVES 4

3 skinless, boneless chicken breasts, weighing 1 lb/450 g in total, cut into bite-size pieces

2 tsp soy sauce

¼ tsp white pepper

2 tbsp peanut oil, plus extra for deep-frying

1¾ oz/50 g thin rice noodles

½ head Chinese cabbage, thinly sliced diagonally

3 scallions, green parts included, sliced diagonally

¼ cup almonds with skin, sliced lengthwise

sesame seeds, to garnish (optional)

dressing

5 tbsp olive oil

3 tbsp rice vinegar

3 tbsp light soy sauce

a few drops sesame oil

salt and pepper

Sprinkle the chicken with the soy sauce and white pepper. To make the dressing, whisk the dressing ingredients together in a separate bowl.

Heat a wok over high heat, then add the 2 tablespoons of peanut oil. Stir-fry the chicken for 4–5 minutes, until brown and crisp. Drain on paper towels and let cool. Wipe out the wok.

Pour enough peanut oil for deep-frying into the wok. Heat until almost smoking, then fry a few noodles at a time, until puffed up and crisp. Drain on paper towels.

Arrange the Chinese cabbage in a shallow serving dish. Place the noodles in a pile on top of the leaves, on one side of the dish. Arrange the chicken, scallions, and almonds in the remaining space. Whisk the dressing again and pour over the salad. Dress with the sesame seeds, if using, and serve immediately.

BANG BANG
CHICKEN SALAD

To make the dressing, put the peanut butter into a heatproof bowl. Set the bowl over a pan of simmering water and stir until the peanut butter has melted. Stir in the chili sauce, soy sauce, and rice vinegar. Remove from the heat and gradually stir in the sunflower and peanut oils to make a dressing with a smooth pouring consistency.

Put the Chinese cabbage leaves on a serving platter and top with the carrots, cucumber, and bean sprouts. Top with the shredded chicken and spoon the warm dressing over it. Sprinkle with the sesame seeds and peanuts and serve immediately.

SERVES 4

8 oz/225 g Chinese cabbage leaves, coarsely torn

2 carrots, cut into thin sticks

½ cucumber, seeded and cut into thin sticks

1 cup bean sprouts

14 oz/400 g cooked boneless chicken breasts, shredded

1 tbsp toasted sesame seeds

1 tbsp salted peanuts, chopped

dressing

4 tbsp smooth peanut butter

2 tbsp sweet chili sauce

1 tbsp soy sauce

1 tbsp rice vinegar

1 tbsp sunflower oil

1 tbsp roasted peanut oil

GINGERED CHICKEN SALAD

Cut the chicken into large cubes, each about 1 inch/2.5 cm. Mix the scallions, ginger, garlic, and 2 tablespoons of oil together in a shallow dish and add the chicken. Cover and let marinate for at least 3 hours. Lift the meat out of the marinade and set aside.

Heat a wok over medium–high heat, then add the remaining oil. Cook the onion for 1–2 minutes, then add the rest of the vegetables except the cucumber. Cook for 2–3 minutes, until just tender. Add the cucumber, half the soy sauce, the sugar, and the basil and mix gently.

Prepare the noodles according to the package directions and drain well. Sprinkle the remaining soy sauce over them and arrange on plates. Top with the cooked vegetables.

Add a little more oil to the wok, if necessary, and cook the chicken over a high heat until browned on all sides. Arrange the chicken cubes on top of the salad and serve hot or warm.

SERVES 4

4 skinless, boneless chicken breasts

4 scallions, chopped

1-inch/2.5-cm piece ginger, finely chopped

4 garlic cloves, crushed

3 tbsp vegetable or peanut oil, plus extra for frying, if needed

1 onion, sliced

1 cup baby corn, halved

2 cups snow peas, halved lengthwise

1 red bell pepper, seeded and sliced

3-inch/7.5-cm piece cucumber, peeled, seeded, and sliced

4 tbsp Thai soy sauce

1 tbsp jaggery or light brown sugar

few Thai basil leaves

6 oz/175 g fine egg noodles

NOODLE BASKETS WITH CHICKEN SALAD

SERVES 4

peanut or corn oil, for deep-frying

9 oz/250 g fresh fine or medium
  egg noodles

chicken lime salad

6 tbsp sour cream

6 tbsp mayonnaise

1-inch/2.5-cm piece fresh ginger,
  grated

grated rind and juice of 1 lime

4 skinless, boneless chicken
  thighs, poached and cooled,
  then cut into thin strips

1 carrot, grated

1 cucumber, cut in half lengthwise,
  seeded, and sliced

1 tbsp finely chopped fresh
  cilantro

1 tbsp finely chopped fresh mint

1 tbsp finely chopped fresh
  flat-leaf parsley

salt and pepper

To shape the noodle baskets, you will need a special set of 2 long-handled wire baskets that clip inside each other, available from specialty kitchen stores. Dip the larger wire basket in oil, then line it completely and evenly with one-quarter of the noodles. Dip the smaller wire basket in oil, then position it inside the larger basket and clip it into position.

Heat the oil in a wok to 350°F/180°C, or until a cube of bread browns in 30 seconds. Lower the baskets into the oil and deep-fry for 2–3 minutes, or until the noodles are golden brown. Remove the baskets from the oil and drain on paper towels. Unclip the 2 wire baskets and carefully remove the small one. Use a palette knife, if necessary, to pry the noodle basket from the wire frame. Repeat to make 3 more baskets. Set aside to cool.

To make the salad, combine the sour cream, mayonnaise, ginger, and lime rind. Gradually add the lime juice until you get the flavor you like. Stir in the chicken, carrot, and cucumber and season to taste with salt and pepper. Cover and let chill.

To serve, stir in the herbs and spoon the salad into the noodle baskets.

CAJUN CHICKEN SALAD

Make 3 diagonal slashes across each chicken breast. Put the chicken into a shallow dish and sprinkle all over with the Cajun seasoning. Cover and let chill for at least 30 minutes.

When ready to cook, brush a stove-top grill pan with the corn oil, if using. Heat over high heat until very hot and a few drops of water sprinkled into the pan sizzle immediately. Add the chicken and cook for 7–8 minutes on each side, or until thoroughly cooked. If still slightly pink in the center, cook a little longer. Remove the chicken and set aside.

Add the mango slices to the pan and cook for 2 minutes on each side. Remove and set aside.

Meanwhile, arrange the salad greens in a salad bowl and sprinkle over the onion, beet, radishes, and walnut halves.

To make the dressing, place all the ingredients in a screw-top jar and shake vigorously until they are well blended. Pour over the salad.

Arrange the mango and the salad on the serving plate, top with the chicken breast, and sprinkle with sesame seeds.

SERVES 4

4 skinless, boneless chicken breasts, about 5 oz/140 g each

4 tsp Cajun seasoning

2 tsp corn oil (optional)

1 ripe mango, peeled, seeded, and cut into thick slices

7 oz/200 g package mixed salad greens

1 red onion, halved and thinly sliced

1 cup cooked, diced beet

¾ cup sliced radishes

scant ½ cup walnut halves

sesame seeds, to garnish

dressing

4 tbsp walnut oil

1–2 tsp Dijon mustard

1 tbsp lemon juice

salt and pepper

BBQ CHICKEN SALAD

Put the oil, tomato sauce, honey, Worcestershire sauce, and mustard powder into a shallow bowl and mix together well. Season with salt and pepper. Add the chicken and turn to coat in the marinade. Cover and let marinate in the refrigerator for 3–4 hours or overnight.

Preheat the oven to 400°F/200°C. Put the chicken on a rack set over a roasting pan. Spoon any remaining marinade over it and roast in the oven for 40–45 minutes, until cooked through and lightly charred in places. Let cool for 5 minutes.

Divide the lettuce leaves among 4 serving plates. Sprinkle with the carrots, corn, and bell pepper. To make the dressing, combine the sour cream and snipped chives in a small bowl and season with salt and pepper.

Thickly slice each chicken portion and arrange on the salads. Serve with the sour cream dressing and garnish with fresh chives, if using.

SERVES 4

1 tbsp olive oil

4 tbsp tomato sauce

1 tbsp honey

1 tbsp Worcestershire sauce

1 tsp mustard powder

4 boneless chicken breasts (with skin), about 5 oz/140 g each

4 Boston lettuce, separated into leaves

4 carrots, coarsely grated

6 tbsp canned corn kernels, drained

½ red bell pepper, seeded and thinly sliced

fresh chives, to garnish (optional)

dressing

6 tbsp sour cream

2 tbsp snipped fresh chives

salt and pepper

CHICKEN FAJITA SALAD

SERVES 4

1 lb/450 g skinless, boneless chicken breasts, sliced

2 tbsp lime juice

2 tbsp olive oil

1 tsp each pepper, dried oregano, and mild chili powder

1 onion, sliced into thin wedges

1 red bell pepper, seeded and thickly sliced

7 oz/200 g package mixed salad greens

lime slices and sour cream, to serve

avocado salsa

1 ripe avocado, peeled, pitted, and finely diced

2 ripe tomatoes, finely chopped

1 tbsp chopped fresh cilantro

1 tbsp lime juice

salt and pepper

To make the salsa, put the avocado into a small bowl and stir in the tomatoes, cilantro, and lime juice. Season with salt and pepper. Cover the surface closely with plastic wrap and chill in the refrigerator.

Put the chicken into a bowl. Add the lime juice, oil, pepper, oregano, and chili powder. Toss to coat. Cover and let marinate at room temperature for 1 hour.

Heat a cast-iron grill pan until very hot and add the chicken slices. Cook for 5–6 minutes, turning occasionally, until the chicken is cooked through and charred in places. Remove from the pan and keep warm. Add the onion and bell pepper to the pan and cook, turning once, for 3–4 minutes, until just tender.

Divide the salad greens among 4 serving plates and top with the chicken, onion, and bell pepper. Serve immediately with the avocado salsa, lime slices, and sour cream.

HONEY & CHICKEN PASTA SALAD

To make the dressing, whisk the dressing ingredients together in a bowl.

Bring a large pan of lightly salted water to a boil. Add the pasta and return to a boil. Cook for 10–12 minutes, until just tender.

Meanwhile, heat the oil in a large skillet. Add the onion and garlic and cook for 5 minutes. Add the chicken and cook, stirring frequently, for 3–4 minutes, until just cooked through. Stir the mustard and honey into the pan and cook for another 2–3 minutes, until the chicken and onion are golden brown and sticky.

Drain the pasta and transfer to a serving bowl. Pour the dressing over it and toss well. Stir in the chicken and onion and let cool.

Gently stir the tomatoes and mizuna into the pasta. Serve garnished with the thyme leaves.

SERVES 4

9 oz/250 g dried pasta twirls, such as fusilli

2 tbsp olive oil

1 onion, thinly sliced

1 garlic clove, crushed

14 oz/400 g skinless, boneless chicken breasts, thinly sliced

2 tbsp whole-grain mustard

2 tbsp honey

10 cherry tomatoes, halved

handful of mizuna or arugula leaves

fresh thyme leaves, to garnish

dressing

3 tbsp olive oil

1 tbsp sherry vinegar

2 tsp honey

1 tbsp fresh thyme leaves

salt and pepper

BRAISED
CHICKEN SALAD

Preheat the oven to 350°F/180°C. Heat the olive oil in an ovenproof casserole over medium–high heat. Add the chicken and fry for 15 minutes, turning, until golden all over. Pour in the wine and simmer for 2 minutes, then add the onion, carrot, celery, and bay leaf. Season with salt and pepper. Cover tightly and transfer to the oven. Bake for 45–50 minutes, turning every 20 minutes, until the juices from the thickest part of the thigh run clear when pierced with a skewer. Discard the liquid and solids. When cool enough to handle, remove and discard the skin. Strip the meat from the bone, slicing any large chunks into bite-size pieces.

Arrange the chicken in a dish to marinate. Sprinkle with a little salt, a few peppercorns, and the bay leaves. Pour in enough oil to generously coat. Cover tightly with plastic wrap and marinate in the refrigerator for 1–2 days.

Remove the chicken from the refrigerator 2 hours before serving. Place in a colander set over a bowl to drain, and let stand until the oil has liquefied.

To make the salad, chop the leaves as desired. Combine the spinach, celery, and endive in a large serving dish. Toss with salt, enough oil from the chicken to just coat the leaves, and the wine vinegar. Arrange the chicken on top, discarding the peppercorns and bay leaves. Sprinkle with the balsamic vinegar before serving.

SERVES 4

3 tbsp olive oil

1 chicken, weighing about
  3 lb/1.3 kg

scant 1 cup dry white wine

1 onion, chopped

1 carrot, chopped

1 celery stalk, chopped

1 fresh bay leaf

salt and pepper

marinade

1 tsp black peppercorns

4 fresh bay leaves

½ cup olive oil

salad

5½ oz/150 g baby spinach leaves

5 tender celery stalks

1 head endive

1 tsp wine vinegar

1 tsp balsamic vinegar

CHICKEN, RAISIN & PINE NUT SALAD

SERVES 6–8

4 large skinless, boneless chicken breasts, about 1 lb 5 oz/600 g in total

5 tbsp olive oil

1 garlic clove, finely chopped

1 cup pine nuts

generous ⅓ cup extra virgin olive oil

1 small bunch fresh flat-leaf parsley, finely chopped

salt and pepper

dressing

¼ cup red wine vinegar

2 tbsp superfine sugar

1 bay leaf

rind of 1 lemon

scant 1 cup seedless raisins

To make the dressing, put the vinegar, sugar, bay leaf, and lemon rind in a pan and bring to a boil, then remove from the heat. Stir in the raisins and let cool.

When the dressing is cool, slice the chicken breasts widthwise into very thin slices. Heat the olive oil in a large skillet, then add the chicken slices and cook over medium heat, stirring occasionally, for 8–10 minutes, or until lightly browned and tender.

Add the garlic and pine nuts and cook, stirring constantly and shaking the skillet, for 1 minute, or until the pine nuts are golden brown. Season to taste with salt and pepper.

Pour the cooled dressing into a large bowl, discarding the bay leaf and lemon rind. Add the extra virgin olive oil and whisk together. Season to taste with salt and pepper. Add the chicken mixture and parsley and toss together. Turn the salad into a serving dish and serve warm or, if serving cold, cover and chill in the refrigerator for 2–3 hours before serving.

TURKEY COUSCOUS SALAD

Put the couscous into a large heatproof bowl. Pour in enough boiling water to cover. Stir well, cover, and let soak for about 15 minutes, until all the liquid has been absorbed. Use a fork to break up any clumps and stir in 3 tablespoons of the olive oil and the vinegar. Season with plenty of salt and pepper.

Heat the remaining oil in a large skillet and add the turkey and harissa paste. Cook, turning frequently, for 3 minutes, until the turkey is no longer pink. Add the zucchini and onion to the skillet and cook, stirring occasionally, for another 10–12 minutes, until the turkey and vegetables are golden brown and tender.

Stir the turkey and vegetables into the couscous with the apricots and pine nuts. Let cool for 10 minutes, then stir in the chopped cilantro and adjust the seasoning to taste. Serve piled into bowls and garnished with chopped cilantro.

SERVES 4

$1\frac{1}{3}$ cups couscous

5 tbsp olive oil

3 tbsp red wine vinegar

12 oz/350 g turkey breast fillet, cubed

1 tsp harissa paste

$1\frac{1}{3}$ cups diced zucchini

1 onion, chopped

½ cup plumped dried apricots, chopped

2 tbsp toasted pine nuts

2 tbsp chopped fresh cilantro, plus extra to garnish

salt and pepper

TURKEY & RICE SALAD

Set aside 3 tablespoons of the chicken stock and bring the remainder to a boil in a large pan. Add the rice and cook for 30 minutes, or until tender. Drain and let cool slightly.

Meanwhile, heat 1 tablespoon of the oil in a preheated wok or skillet. Stir-fry the turkey over medium heat for 3–4 minutes, or until cooked through. Using a slotted spoon, transfer the turkey to a dish. Add the snow peas and mushrooms to the wok and stir-fry for 1 minute. Add the reserved stock, bring to a boil, then reduce the heat, cover, and let simmer for 3–4 minutes. Transfer the vegetables to the dish and let cool slightly.

Thoroughly mix the rice, turkey, snow peas, mushrooms, nuts, cilantro, and garlic chives together, then season to taste with salt and pepper. Drizzle with the remaining corn oil and the vinegar and garnish with fresh garlic chives. Serve warm.

SERVES 4

4 cups chicken stock

scant 1 cup mixed long-grain and wild rice

2 tbsp corn oil

8 oz/225 g skinless, boneless turkey breast, trimmed of all visible fat and cut into thin strips

2 cups snow peas

4 oz/115 g oyster mushrooms, torn into pieces

¼ cup finely chopped, shelled pistachio nuts

2 tbsp chopped fresh cilantro

1 tbsp snipped fresh garlic chives

1 tbsp balsamic vinegar

salt and pepper

fresh garlic chives, to garnish

ROAST DUCK
SALAD

SERVES 4

2 duck breasts

2 Boston lettuce, shredded

1 cup bean sprouts

1 yellow bell pepper, seeded and
   cut into thin strips

½ cucumber, seeded and
   cut into short thin sticks

shredded lime zest and shredded
   coconut, toasted, to garnish

dressing

juice of 2 limes

3 tbsp Thai fish sauce

1 tbsp brown sugar

2 tsp sweet chili sauce

1 inch/2.5 cm fresh ginger,
   finely grated

3 tbsp chopped fresh mint

3 tbsp chopped fresh basil

Preheat the oven to 400°F/200°C. Place the duck breasts
on a rack set over a roasting pan and roast in the oven for
20–30 minutes, or until cooked as desired and the skin is crisp.
Remove from the oven and set aside to cool.

   In a large bowl, combine the lettuce, bean sprouts, bell pepper,
and cucumber. Cut the cooled duck into slices and add to the
salad. Mix well.

   To make the dressing, whisk the dressing ingredients together
in a separate bowl. Add the dressing to the salad and toss well.

   Turn the salad out onto a serving platter and garnish with the
shredded lime zest and coconut before serving.

WARM DUCK, SHALLOT & ORANGE SALAD

Preheat the oven to 400°F/200°C. Halve and squeeze the juice from 1 of the oranges. Using a serrated knife, remove all the peel and white pith from the other orange, then halve and thinly slice.

Season the duck fillets with salt and pepper. Heat a large heavy skillet and add the duck fillets, skin side down. Cook over medium–high heat for 5–6 minutes, until the skin is golden brown. Turn over and cook for another minute. Transfer the duck fillets to a shallow roasting pan and roast in the oven for 10 minutes, or a little longer if you prefer the duck well done.

Add the shallots to the skillet and turn to coat in the duck fat. Cook gently for 7–8 minutes, until golden and tender. Remove with a slotted spoon and keep warm. Pour the orange juice into the skillet and bring to a boil. Whisk in the sugar, oil, and vinegar and simmer for 2–3 minutes, until just syrupy. Season to taste with salt and pepper.

Put the spinach, Swiss chard leaves, and orange slices onto 4 serving plates. Slice each duck fillet and place on top of the salad with the shallots. Spoon the warm dressing over them and serve immediately.

SERVES 4

2 large oranges

4 duck breast fillets, about 6 oz/175 g each

12 small shallots, halved

1 tbsp sugar

2 tbsp olive oil

1 tbsp red wine vinegar

1¾ cups baby spinach leaves

1¾ cups baby red Swiss chard leaves

salt and pepper

DUCK & RADISH SALAD

Put each duck breast between sheets of parchment paper or plastic wrap. Use a meat mallet or rolling pin to beat them out and flatten them slightly.

Sprinkle the flour onto a large plate and season with salt and pepper. Beat together the egg and water in a shallow bowl, then sprinkle the sesame seeds onto a separate plate.

Dip the duck breasts first into the seasoned flour, then into the egg mixture and finally into the sesame seeds to coat the duck evenly.

Heat a wok or large skillet over medium heat and add the sesame oil. When hot, add the duck breasts and fry for about 8 minutes, turning once. To test whether they are cooked, insert a sharp knife into the thickest part—the juices should run clear. Lift them out and drain on paper towels.

To make the dressing, whisk the dressing ingredients together in a separate bowl.

Arrange the Chinese cabbage, celery, and radishes on a serving plate. Slice the duck breasts thinly and place on top of the salad.

Drizzle with the dressing and garnish with fresh basil leaves. Serve at once.

SERVES 4

12 oz boneless duck breasts

2 tbsp all-purpose flour

1 egg

2 tbsp water

2 tbsp sesame seeds

3 tbsp sesame oil

½ head Chinese cabbage, shredded

3 celery stalks, sliced finely

8 radishes, trimmed and halved

fresh basil leaves, to garnish

salt and pepper

dressing

finely grated peel of 1 lime

2 tbsp lime juice

2 tbsp olive oil

1 tbsp light soy sauce

1 tbsp chopped fresh basil

DUCK SALAD WITH SWEET CHILI DRESSING

SERVES 4

2 duck legs, about 6 oz/175 g each

1 tsp five-spice powder

2¾ cups sugar snap peas

1 small iceberg lettuce,
   finely shredded

2 celery stalks, very thinly sliced

6 scallions, finely shredded

dressing

1 tbsp sunflower oil

3 tbsp sweet chili sauce

1 tbsp rice vinegar

salt and pepper

Preheat the oven to 400°F/200°C. Put the duck legs into a roasting pan and pour 1¼ cups boiling water over the skin. Drain off the water and pat the skins dry with paper towels.

Rub the five-spice powder into the duck skin. Roast the duck legs in the oven for 1¼–1½ hours, until cooked through with golden crispy skin. Let cool for 10 minutes.

To make the dressing, whisk the dressing ingredients together in a separate bowl.

Bring a small pan of water to a boil and add the sugar snap peas. Cook for 2 minutes, then drain and refresh under cold running water. Thinly slice the sugar snap peas lengthwise and put them into a bowl with the lettuce, celery, and nearly all the scallions. Toss well to mix.

Peel off the crispy skin from the roast duck and cut it into thin strips. Using 2 forks, pull and shred all the duck flesh from the bones.

Transfer the salad to a platter and top with the shredded duck and crispy skin. Drizzle the dressing over it and garnish with the rest of the scallions. Serve immediately.

DUCK & NOODLE SALAD WITH PEANUT SAUCE

Preheat the broiler. Cut the carrots, celery, and cucumber into thin strips and set aside.

Broil the duck breasts for about 5 minutes on each side, until cooked through. Let cool.

Meanwhile, heat all the ingredients for the sauce in a small pan until combined and the sugar has dissolved completely. Stir until smooth.

Slice the duck breasts. Divide the noodles among 3 serving bowls. Place the reserved carrots, celery, and cucumber on top of the noodles, arrange the duck slices on top, and drizzle with the sauce. Serve immediately.

SERVES 3

2 carrots, peeled

2 celery stalks

1 cucumber

3 duck breasts, about
   5 oz/140 g each

12 oz/350 g rice noodles, cooked
   according to directions on
   package, rinsed, and drained

peanut sauce

2 garlic cloves, crushed

2 tbsp dark brown sugar

2 tbsp peanut butter

2 tbsp coconut cream

2 tbsp soy sauce

2 tbsp rice vinegar

2 tbsp sesame oil

½ tsp pepper

½ tsp Chinese five-spice powder

½ tsp ground ginger

FISH & SEAFOOD

SALAD NIÇOISE

Heat a ridged, cast-iron grill pan over high heat until you can feel the heat rising from the surface. Brush the tuna steaks with oil, place them, oiled side down, on the hot pan, and cook for 2 minutes. Lightly brush the top sides of the tuna steaks with more oil. Use a pair of tongs to turn the tuna steaks over, then season to taste with salt and pepper. Continue cooking for another 2 minutes for rare or up to 4 minutes for well done. Let cool.

Meanwhile, bring a pan of salted water to a boil. Add the beans to the pan and return to a boil, then boil for 3 minutes, or until tender-crisp. Drain the beans and immediately transfer them to a large bowl. Pour over the vinaigrette and stir together, then let the beans cool in the dressing.

To serve, line a platter with lettuce leaves. Lift the beans out of the bowl, leaving the excess dressing behind, and pile them in the center of the platter. Break the tuna into large pieces and arrange it over the beans. Arrange the hard-cooked eggs and the tomatoes around the side. Arrange the anchovy fillets over the salad, then scatter with the olives. Drizzle over the remaining dressing in the bowl and serve.

SERVES 4

2 tuna steaks, about
 ³⁄₄ inch/2 cm thick

olive oil, for brushing

9 oz/250 g green beans, trimmed

½ cup vinaigrette or garlic
 vinaigrette dressing

2 hearts lettuce, leaves separated

3 large hard-cooked eggs,
 cut into quarters

2 juicy vine-ripened tomatoes,
 cut into wedges

1³⁄₄ oz/50 g anchovy fillets in oil,
 drained

½ cup Niçoise olives, pitted

salt and pepper

CARAMELIZED TUNA SALAD

To make the dressing, heat a small wok over high heat. Add the oil and fry the ginger and chile for a few seconds. Add the soy sauce, Thai fish sauce, and tamarind paste. Stir for 30 seconds, then add the sugar and stir until dissolved. Remove the wok from the heat and set aside.

Rinse the bean sprouts in boiling water and drain. Blot dry with paper towels. Peel the cucumber, halve lengthwise, and scoop out the seeds. Thinly slice the flesh diagonally.

Put the bean sprouts, cucumber, cilantro, and mint leaves in a bowl. Season with a pinch of salt and a few drops of sesame oil. Toss to combine, then divide between individual serving plates.

Heat a large wok over high heat, then add the sesame and peanut oils. Quickly stir-fry the tuna, turning with tongs, until colored on the outside but still slightly red in the middle. Arrange the tuna chunks on top of the salad.

Reheat the dressing, thinning with a spoonful of water if necessary, and pour over the tuna. Sprinkle with the crushed peanuts and serve at once.

SERVES 4

2 cups fresh bean sprouts

4-inch/10-cm piece cucumber

1½ cups cilantro leaves

1½ cups mint leaves

1 tsp sesame oil, plus a few drops for drizzling

1 tbsp peanut oil

1 lb/450 g fresh tuna, cut into 1-inch/2.5-cm chunks

salt

salted roasted peanuts, crushed, to garnish

dressing

2 tsp canola oil

1 tsp finely chopped fresh ginger

½–1 small fresh red chile, seeded and finely chopped

4 tbsp light soy sauce

1 tbsp Thai fish sauce

1 tbsp tamarind paste

⅓ cup brown sugar

TUNA, LENTIL & POTATO SALAD

SERVES 4

1 cup Puy or brown lentils

2 tbsp olive oil, plus extra
for brushing

10½ oz/300 g baby new potatoes,
washed

1 head Boston lettuce

4 fresh tuna steaks,
about 3½ oz/100 g each

12 small cherry tomatoes, halved

2 cups arugula leaves

salt and pepper

dressing

5 tbsp fruity olive oil

1 tbsp balsamic vinegar

2 tsp red wine vinegar

1 tsp smooth Dijon mustard

1 tsp light brown sugar

Cook the lentils in a saucepan of boiling water for 25 minutes,
or until tender. Drain, then tip into a bowl and stir in the oil.

Meanwhile, cook the potatoes in a separate saucepan of lightly
salted water for 15 minutes, or until just tender.

Break off the outer lettuce leaves and cut the heart into
8 even pieces. Arrange on 4 individual serving plates.

To make the dressing, place all the ingredients in a screw-top
jar and shake vigorously until they are well blended.

When the potatoes are nearly cooked, lightly brush a ridged
grill pan with oil and heat over high heat. When very hot, add
the tuna steaks and cook for 1½ minutes on each side to sear.
Remove to a cutting board and cut each steak into 6 chunks.

Drain the potatoes and coarsely chop any larger ones. Arrange
with the lentils, tuna, and tomatoes on the serving plates, then
sprinkle over the arugula leaves and spoon over the dressing.
Serve immediately.

TUNA & TWO-BEAN SALAD

To make the dressing, place all the ingredients in a screw-top jar and shake vigorously until they are well blended.

Bring a pan of lightly salted water to a boil. Add the green beans and cook for 3 minutes. Add the white beans and cook for another 4 minutes, until the green beans are tender-crisp and the white beans are heated through. Drain well and add to the bowl with the dressing and scallions. Toss together.

To cook the tuna, heat a stove-top ridged grill pan over high heat. Lightly brush the tuna steaks with oil, then season to taste with salt and pepper. Cook the steaks for 2 minutes, then turn over and cook on the other side for another 2 minutes for rare or up to 4 minutes for well done.

Remove the tuna from the grill pan and let rest for 2 minutes, or alternatively let stand until completely cool. When ready to serve, add the tomatoes to the bean mixture and toss lightly. Line a serving platter with the lettuce leaves and pile on the bean salad. Place the tuna over the top. Serve warm or at room temperature, garnished with the herbs.

SERVES 4

7 oz/200 g green beans

14 oz/400 g canned small white beans, such as cannellini, rinsed and drained

4 scallions, finely chopped

2 fresh tuna steaks, about 8 oz/225 g each and ¾ inch/2 cm thick

olive oil, for brushing

1⅔ cups halved cherry tomatoes

handful lettuce leaves

salt and pepper

fresh mint and flat-leaf parsley sprigs, to garnish

dressing

handful fresh mint leaves, shredded

handful fresh flat-leaf parsley leaves, chopped

1 garlic clove, crushed

4 tbsp extra virgin olive oil

1 tbsp red wine vinegar

TUNA & HERBED PASTA SALAD

Preheat the broiler to high. Bring a large pan of lightly salted water to a boil. Add the pasta, return to a boil, and cook for 8–10 minutes until tender but still firm to the bite, or according to the package directions.

Meanwhile, put the bell pepper quarters under the preheated broiler and cook for 10–12 minutes, until the skins begin to blacken. Transfer to a plastic bag, seal, and set aside.

Bring a separate pan of water to a boil, add the asparagus, and blanch for 4 minutes. Drain and plunge into cold water, then drain again. Remove the pasta from the heat, drain, and set aside to cool. Remove the bell pepper quarters from the bag and peel off the skins. Slice the bell pepper into strips.

To make the dressing, put all the dressing ingredients in a large bowl and stir together well. Add the pasta, bell pepper strips, asparagus, onion, tomatoes, and tuna. Toss together gently, then divide among serving bowls. Garnish with basil sprigs and serve.

SERVES 4

7 oz/200 g dried pasta twirls, such as fusilli

1 red bell pepper, seeded and cut into quarters

5½ oz/150 g asparagus spears

1 red onion, sliced

4 tomatoes, sliced

7 oz/200 g canned tuna in brine, drained and flaked

salt

dressing

6 tbsp basil-flavored oil or extra virgin olive oil

3 tbsp white wine vinegar

1 tbsp lime juice

1 tsp mustard

1 tsp honey

4 tbsp chopped fresh basil, plus extra sprigs to garnish

TOMATO, SALMON & SHRIMP SALAD

SERVES 4

8 cherry or baby plum tomatoes

handful lettuce leaves

4 ripe tomatoes, coarsely chopped

3½ oz/100 g smoked salmon

7 oz/200 g large cooked shrimp,
   thawed if frozen

dressing

1 tbsp Dijon mustard

2 tsp superfine sugar

2 tsp red wine vinegar

2 tbsp medium olive oil

few fresh dill sprigs,
   plus extra to garnish

pepper

Halve most of the cherry tomatoes. Place the lettuce leaves around the edge of a shallow bowl and add all of the tomatoes and cherry tomatoes. Using scissors, snip the smoked salmon into strips and sprinkle over the tomatoes, then add the shrimp.

To make the dressing, mix the mustard, sugar, vinegar, and oil together in a small bowl, then tear most of the dill sprigs into it. Mix well and pour over the salad. Toss well to coat the salad with the dressing. Snip the remaining dill over the top and season to taste with pepper.

SMOKED SALMON & ARUGULA SALAD

Shred the arugula and arrange in 4 individual bowls. Sprinkle over the chopped parsley and scallions.

Halve, peel, and pit the avocados and cut into thin slices or small chunks. Brush with the lemon juice to prevent discoloration, then divide among the salad bowls. Mix together gently. Cut the smoked salmon into strips and sprinkle over the top.

To make the dressing, whisk the dressing ingredients together in a separate bowl. Spoon some of the mayonnaise dressing on top of each salad and garnish with parsley sprigs.

SERVES 4

2½ cups wild arugula leaves

1 tbsp chopped fresh flat-leaf parsley

2 scallions, finely diced

2 large avocados

1 tbsp lemon juice

9 oz/250 g smoked salmon

dressing

⅔ cup mayonnaise

2 tbsp lime juice

finely grated rind of 1 lime

1 tbsp chopped fresh flat-leaf parsley, plus extra sprigs to garnish

TERIYAKI SALMON SALAD

Put half the shredded scallions into a small bowl of cold water with a couple of ice cubes. Let stand in the refrigerator for at least 1 hour, until the scallions are curly.

Put the salmon fillets into a shallow dish and pour the teriyaki sauce over them. Cover and let marinate at room temperature for 30 minutes.

Cook the noodles in a large pan of lightly salted boiling water for 3 minutes, until just tender. Drain well and refresh under cold running water. Transfer to a bowl.

Heat the oil in a wok and add the ginger, bell pepper, carrots, and remaining scallions. Stir-fry for 1 minute. Add the sesame seeds and stir-fry for another minute. Cool for 10 minutes, then add to the noodles with the vinegar, and toss well to mix. Season with salt and pepper.

Heat a nonstick skillet and add the salmon fillets, skin side down. Cook for 1 minute on each side, until browned. Pour in the teriyaki marinade. Reduce the heat and cook for another 3–4 minutes on each side, until just cooked through.

Divide the noodle salad among 4 serving plates and top each with a salmon fillet. Drain the scallion curls and pat dry with paper towels. Put them on top of the salmon fillets and serve with lime wedges.

SERVES 4

6 scallions, finely shredded

4 salmon fillets (with skin), about 4 oz/115 g each

4 tbsp teriyaki sauce

8 oz/225 g thread egg noodles

2 tsp toasted sesame oil

1 tsp grated fresh ginger

1 green bell pepper, seeded and finely shredded

2 carrots, finely shredded

2 tbsp sesame seeds

2 tbsp rice vinegar

salt and pepper

lime wedges, to serve

WARM SALMON & MANGO SALAD

SERVES 4

8 sungold or red cherry tomatoes

3 oz/85 g salmon fillets, skinned and cut into small cubes

1 large ripe mango, cut into small chunks (about ¾ cup)

2 tbsp orange juice

1 tbsp soy sauce

4 cups assorted salad greens

½ cucumber, trimmed and sliced into thin sticks

6 scallions, trimmed and chopped

dressing

4 tbsp low-fat plain yogurt

1 tsp soy sauce

1 tbsp finely grated orange rind

Cut half the tomatoes in half and set aside.

Thread the salmon with the whole tomatoes and half the mango chunks onto 4 kebab sticks. Mix the orange juice and soy sauce together in a small bowl and brush over the kebabs. Let marinate for 15 minutes, brushing with the remaining orange juice mixture at least once more.

Arrange the salad greens on a serving platter with the reserved halved tomatoes, mango chunks, the cucumber sticks, and scallions.

Preheat the broiler to high and line the broiler rack with foil. To make the dressing, whisk the dressing ingredients together in a separate bowl.

Place the salmon kebabs on the broiler rack, brush again with the marinade, and broil for 5 to 7 minutes, or until the salmon is cooked. Turn the kebabs over halfway through cooking and brush with any remaining marinade.

Divide the prepared salad among 4 plates, top each with a kebab, and then drizzle with the dressing.

SMOKED TROUT, ENDIVE & PEAR SALAD

Toss the sliced pears in the lemon juice to prevent discoloration. Put them into a serving dish with the endive leaves and watercress.

Flake the smoked trout, removing any skin and fine bones. Sprinkle it over the salad with the grapes.

To make the dressing, whisk the dressing ingredients together in a separate bowl. Drizzle the dressing over the salad just before serving. Season with a little more pepper.

SERVES 4

2 ripe red Bartlett pears, cored and sliced

1 tbsp lemon juice

3 heads endive, trimmed and leaves separated

½ bunch watercress, coarse stalks removed

8 oz/225 g smoked trout fillets

½ cup green grapes, halved

dressing

4 tbsp crème fraîche

1 tbsp milk

1 tsp creamed horseradish

2 tsp lemon juice

salt and pepper

CAESAR
SALAD

Bring a small, heavy-bottom pan of water to a boil.

Meanwhile, heat 4 tablespoons of the olive oil in a heavy-bottom skillet. Add the garlic and cubed bread and cook, stirring and tossing frequently, for 4–5 minutes, or until the bread is crispy and golden all over. Remove from the skillet with a slotted spoon and drain on paper towels.

Add the egg to the boiling water and cook for 1 minute, then remove from the pan and set aside.

Arrange the salad greens in a salad bowl. Mix the remaining olive oil and lemon juice together, then season to taste with salt and pepper. Crack the egg into the dressing and whisk to blend. Pour the dressing over the salad greens, toss well, then add the croutons and chopped anchovies and toss the salad again. Sprinkle with Parmesan cheese shavings and serve.

SERVES 4

²⁄₃ cup olive oil

2 garlic cloves

5 slices white bread, crusts removed, cut into ½-inch/1-cm cubes

1 egg

2 romaine lettuce or 3 Boston lettuce

2 tbsp lemon juice

8 canned anchovy fillets, drained and coarsely chopped

fresh Parmesan cheese shavings, to serve

salt and pepper

ANCHOVY & OLIVE SALAD

SERVES 4

handful mixed lettuce leaves

12 cherry tomatoes, halved

20 black olives, pitted and halved

6 canned anchovy fillets, drained
and sliced

1 tbsp chopped fresh oregano

wedges of lemon, to garnish

fresh crusty bread rolls, to serve

dressing

4 tbsp extra virgin olive oil

1 tbsp white wine vinegar

1 tbsp lemon juice

1 tbsp chopped fresh
flat-leaf parsley

salt and pepper

To make the dressing, stir the dressing ingredients together in a bowl.

To assemble the salad, arrange the lettuce leaves in a serving dish. Scatter the cherry tomatoes on top, followed by the olives, anchovies, and oregano. Drizzle over the dressing.

Transfer to individual plates, garnish with lemon wedges, and serve with crusty bread rolls.

WARM MACKEREL & POTATO SALAD

Make 3–4 diagonal slashes in the skin of each mackerel fillet and put them into a dish. Combine the coarsely ground pepper, lemon rind and juice, and oil and pour the mixture over the fillets. Cover and let marinate at room temperature for 20 minutes.

Preheat the broiler. Cook the mackerel fillets under the broiler, turning once, for 7–8 minutes, until just cooked through.

Meanwhile, cook the potatoes in a pan of lightly salted boiling water for 10–12 minutes, until tender.

To make the dressing, whisk the dressing ingredients together in a separate bowl.

Drain the potatoes and mix gently with the scallions and half the dressing. Divide among 4 serving plates and add the arugula leaves. Top each salad with a hot mackerel fillet and drizzle the rest of the dressing over them. Garnish with fresh dill sprigs and serve.

SERVES 4

4 mackerel fillets,
    about 5 oz/140 g each

1 tsp coarsely ground black
    pepper

thinly pared rind and juice
    of 1 small lemon

1 tbsp extra virgin olive oil

1 lb/450 g new potatoes, sliced

4 scallions, thinly sliced

1¼ cups wild arugula leaves

fresh dill sprigs, to garnish

dressing

5 tbsp extra virgin olive oil

2 tbsp white wine vinegar

1 tsp Dijon mustard

pinch of sugar

1 tbsp chopped fresh dill

salt and pepper

SEARED SWORDFISH WITH SALSA

To make the tomato & olive salsa, whisk the olive oil and vinegar together in a bowl large enough to hold all the ingredients. Gently stir in the tomatoes, olives, shallot, and capers with salt and pepper to taste. Cover and chill until required.

Season the swordfish steaks on both sides with salt. Melt the butter with the oil in a skillet large enough to hold the swordfish steaks in a single layer. (If you don't have a large enough pan, cook the steaks in 2 batches.)

Add the swordfish steaks to the pan in a single layer and fry for about another 3 minutes, until golden brown, then carefully turn the fish over and continue frying for about 3 minutes longer until the fish is cooked through and flakes easily. Remove the fish from the pan and set aside to cool completely. Cover and chill for at least 2 hours.

When ready to serve, remove the fish from the refrigerator at least 15 minutes in advance. Stir the basil into the salsa, then adjust the seasoning if necessary. Break the swordfish into large flakes and gently stir into the salsa—be careful to avoid breaking up the fish too much. Arrange the fish salad in 4 bowls, spooning over any of the leftover juices, and serve with crusty bread.

SERVES 4

4 boneless swordfish steaks, about 5 oz/140 g each

½ cup butter

1 tbsp olive oil

fresh crusty bread, to serve

fresh tomato & olive salsa

4 tbsp extra virgin olive oil

1 tbsp red wine vinegar

1 lb 5 oz/600 g ripe, juicy beef tomatoes, cored, seeded, and finely chopped

¾ cup large black olives, pitted and cut in half

1 shallot, finely chopped or thinly sliced

1 tbsp capers in brine, rinsed and dried

salt and pepper

3 tbsp finely shredded fresh basil leaves

SWEET & SOUR FISH SALAD

SERVES 4

8 oz/225 g trout fillets

8 oz/225 g white fish fillets
(such as haddock or cod)

1¼ cups water

1 stem lemongrass

2 lime leaves

1 large red chile

1 bunch scallions,
trimmed and shredded

1 cup diced fresh pineapple

1 small red bell pepper,
seeded and diced

1 bunch watercress,
washed and trimmed

fresh snipped chives, to garnish

dressing

1 tbsp sunflower oil

1 tbsp rice wine vinegar

pinch of chili powder

1 tsp honey

salt and pepper

Rinse the fish, place in a skillet, and pour over the water. Bend the lemongrass in half to bruise it and add to the skillet with the lime leaves. Prick the chile with a fork and add to the pan. Bring to a boil and simmer for 7–8 minutes. Let cool.

Drain the fish fillet thoroughly, then flake the flesh away from the skin and place it in a bowl. Gently stir in the scallions, pineapple, and bell pepper.

Arrange the washed watercress on 4 serving plates and spoon the cooked fish mixture on top.

To make the dressing, mix the dressing ingredients together in a separate bowl. Spoon it over the fish and serve the salad garnished with chives.

149

SPICED FISH SKEWERS & TOMATO SALAD

Put the fish cubes into a shallow bowl. Combine 2 tablespoons of the lime juice and 2 tablespoons of the oil with the chili powder and oregano in a pitcher. Season with salt and pepper and pour the mixture over the fish. Cover and let marinate at room temperature for 1 hour.

Preheat the broiler to medium. Thread the pieces of fish and two lemon wedges onto each skewer and cook the skewers, turning occasionally, for 8–10 minutes, until just cooked.

Meanwhile, combine the tomatoes, onion, and cilantro in a bowl. Whisk the remaining lime juice and oil together with the sugar and mustard. Pour the dressing over the tomatoes and toss well to mix. Season with salt and pepper.

Divide the tomato salad among 4 serving dishes and top each with 2 fish skewers. Serve immediately.

SERVES 4

1 lb/450 g cod loin or monkfish, cut into 1-inch/2.5-cm cubes

3 tbsp lime juice

4 tbsp sunflower oil

2 tsp mild chili powder

1 tsp dried oregano

1 lemon, cut into 8 wedges

16 red cherry tomatoes, halved

16 yellow cherry tomatoes, halved

½ small onion, thinly sliced

2 tbsp coarsely chopped fresh cilantro

½ tsp sugar

1 tsp mild mustard

salt and pepper

SHRIMP & WHITE BEAN SALAD

Put the beans, onion, celery, shrimp, and garlic into a large shallow bowl. Add the lemon juice, 2 tablespoons of the oil, and the chopped parsley. Season lightly with salt and pepper. Stir well, then cover and set aside.

Brush the slices of bread with some of the remaining olive oil. Cook on a hot griddle for 2–3 minutes on each side, until golden, or toast under a hot broiler. Put them on 4 serving plates.

Gently stir the tomatoes and parsley leaves into the salad. Pile the salad onto the hot toasts. Drizzle the rest of the olive oil over the salad, season with a little more pepper, and serve.

SERVES 4

14 oz/400 g canned cannellini beans, drained and rinsed

½ red onion, finely chopped

1 celery stalk, finely diced

10½ oz/300 g cooked, large peeled shrimp with tails intact

1 garlic clove, finely chopped

juice of 1 lemon

5 tbsp extra virgin olive oil

2 tbsp chopped fresh flat-leaf parsley

4 thick slices rustic bread

6 baby plum tomatoes, halved

handful of fresh flat-leaf parsley leaves

salt and pepper

COCONUT SHRIMP SALAD

SERVES 4

1 cup brown basmati rice

½ tsp coriander seeds

2 egg whites, lightly beaten

generous ¾ cup dry unsweetened coconut

24 raw jumbo shrimp, shelled

½ cucumber

4 scallions, thinly sliced lengthwise

1 tsp sesame oil

1 tbsp finely chopped fresh cilantro

Bring a large pan of water to a boil, add the rice, and cook for 25 minutes, or until tender. Drain and keep in a strainer covered with a clean dish towel to absorb the steam.

Meanwhile, soak 8 wooden skewers in cold water for 30 minutes, then drain. Crush the coriander seeds in a mortar with a pestle. Heat a nonstick skillet over medium heat, add the crushed coriander seeds, and cook, turning, until they start to color. Tip onto a plate and set aside.

Put the egg whites into a shallow bowl and the coconut into a separate bowl. Roll each shrimp first in the egg whites, then in the coconut. Thread onto a skewer. Repeat so that each skewer is threaded with 3 coated shrimp.

Preheat the broiler to high. Using a vegetable peeler, peel long strips from the cucumber to create ribbons, put into a strainer to drain, then toss with the scallions and oil in a bowl and set aside.

Cook the shrimp under the preheated broiler for 3–4 minutes on each side, or until slightly browned.

Meanwhile, mix the rice with the toasted coriander seeds and fresh cilantro and divide this and the cucumber salad among the bowls. Serve with the hot shrimp skewers.

LAYERED CRAYFISH SALAD

To make the dressing, mix the dressing ingredients together in a bowl.

Divide the grated carrot among 4 individual bowls. Put the shredded lettuce in a layer on top of the carrots, followed by the cucumber and corn.

Spoon the dressing over the salad and pile the crayfish tails on top. Sprinkle with the cayenne pepper. Garnish with lemon wedges, if using, and serve.

FISH & SEAFOOD

156

SERVES 4

generous ¾ cup grated carrots

1 Boston lettuce, shredded

½ cup drained canned corn kernels

¼ cucumber, diced

6 oz/175 g cooked crayfish tails in brine, thoroughly drained

½ tsp cayenne pepper

lemon wedges, to garnish (optional)

dressing

½ cup mayonnaise

1 tbsp ketchup

dash of Worcestershire sauce

1 tbsp lemon juice

salt and pepper

THAI CRAB
PATTY SALAD

Put the crab, shrimp, lime juice, and curry paste into a food processor and process for a few seconds until finely ground. Add the egg white and chopped cilantro and season well with salt and pepper. Process for a few seconds more until well mixed.

Transfer the mixture to a bowl and, using lightly floured hands, shape into 12 small patties. Coat lightly in the flour. Cover and chill in the refrigerator for 1 hour.

Heat the oil in a large skillet and fry the crab patties, in 2 batches, turning once, for 3–4 minutes, until golden brown. Drain on paper towels.

Put the cucumber, bean sprouts, cress, and cilantro stalks into a bowl and toss with the rice vinegar. Divide among 4 serving plates. Top with the hot crab patties and spoon the chili sauce over them. Serve garnished with cilantro leaves and lime wedges.

SERVES 4

12 oz/350 g canned white crabmeat, drained

5 oz/140 g cooked peeled shrimp

1 tsp lime juice

2 tsp Thai red curry paste

1 tbsp beaten egg white

1 tbsp chopped fresh cilantro

1 tbsp all-purpose flour, plus extra for dusting

sunflower oil, for shallow-frying

½ cucumber, peeled, seeded, and thinly sliced

4 cups bean sprouts

½ cup cress

2 tbsp chopped fresh cilantro stalks

1 tbsp rice vinegar

4 tbsp sweet chili sauce

salt and pepper

fresh cilantro leaves and lime wedges, to garnish

LOBSTER & SUMMER HERB SALAD

SERVES 4–6

1 lb 10 oz–1 lb 12 oz/750–800 g
   freshly cooked lobster meat,
   cut into bite-size chunks

1 large avocado, peeled, pitted,
   and cut into chunky dice

4 ripe but firm tomatoes

9 oz/250 g package mixed herb
   salad greens

1–2 tbsp fruity olive oil

squeeze of lemon juice

salt and pepper

saffron mayonnaise

pinch of saffron threads

1 egg

1 tsp Dijon mustard

1 tbsp white wine vinegar

pinch of salt

1¼ cups sunflower oil

For the mayonnaise, soak the saffron threads in a little warm water. Meanwhile, put the egg, mustard, vinegar, and salt in a food processor or blender and process to combine. With the motor running, slowly trickle in about one-third of the sunflower oil. Once the mixture starts to thicken, add the remaining oil more quickly. When all the oil has been incorporated, add the saffron and its soaking water and process to combine. Add more salt and pepper to taste, then cover and refrigerate until required.

Put the lobster meat and avocado in a bowl. Quarter the tomatoes and remove the seeds. Cut the flesh into fairly chunky dice and add to the bowl. Season the lobster mixture to taste with salt and pepper and gently stir in enough of the mayonnaise to give everything a light coating.

Toss the salad greens with the olive oil and lemon juice. Divide between 4 plates and top with the lobster mixture. Serve immediately.

SEAFOOD
SALAD

Clean the mussels by scrubbing or scraping the shells and pulling out any beards that are attached to them. Discard any with broken shells or any that refuse to close when tapped. Put the mussels in a colander and rinse well under cold running water. Put them in a large pan with a little water and cook, covered, over a high heat, shaking the pan occasionally, for 3–4 minutes, or until the mussels have opened. Discard any mussels that remain closed. Strain the mussels, reserving the cooking liquid. Refresh the mussels under cold running water, drain, and set aside.

Return the reserved cooking liquid to the pan and bring to a boil, add the scallops and squid, and cook for 3 minutes. Remove from the heat and drain. Refresh under cold running water and drain again. Remove the mussels from their shells. Put them in a bowl with the scallops and squid and let cool. Cover with plastic wrap and let chill in the refrigerator for 45 minutes.

Divide the seafood among 4 serving plates and top with the onion. To make the dressing, mix the dressing ingredients together in a separate bowl. Garnish with chopped parsley and serve with lemon wedges.

SERVES 4

9 oz/250 g live mussels

12 oz/350 g live scallops, shucked and cleaned

9 oz/250 g prepared squid, cut into rings and tentacles

1 red onion, halved and finely sliced

chopped fresh flat-leaf parsley, to garnish

lemon wedges, to serve

dressing

4 tbsp extra virgin olive oil

2 tbsp white wine vinegar

1 tbsp lemon juice

1 garlic clove, finely chopped

1 tbsp chopped fresh flat-leaf parsley

salt and pepper

SEAFOOD & SPINACH SALAD

Put the mussels into a large pan with a little water, bring to a boil, and cook over high heat for 4 minutes. Drain and reserve the liquid. Discard any mussels that remain closed. Return the reserved liquid to the pan and bring to a boil. Add the shrimp and scallops and cook for 3 minutes. Drain. Remove the mussels from their shells. Rinse the mussels, shrimp, and scallops in cold water, drain, and put them in a large bowl. Cool, cover with plastic wrap, and chill for 45 minutes. Meanwhile, rinse the baby spinach leaves and transfer them to a pan with 4 tablespoons of water. Cook over high heat for 1 minute, transfer to a strainer, refresh under cold running water, and drain.

To make the dressing, mix the dressing ingredients together in a separate bowl. Arrange the spinach on serving dishes, then scatter over half of the scallions. Top with the mussels, shrimp, and scallops, then scatter over the remaining scallions. Drizzle over the dressing and serve.

SERVES 4

1 lb 2 oz/500 g live mussels,
    soaked and cleaned

3½ oz/100 g shrimp,
    peeled and deveined

12 oz/350 g scallops

1 lb 2 oz/500 g baby
    spinach leaves

3 scallions, trimmed and sliced

dressing

4 tbsp extra virgin olive oil

2 tbsp white wine vinegar

1 tbsp lemon juice

1 tsp finely grated lemon zest

1 garlic clove, chopped

1 tbsp grated fresh ginger

1 small red chile,
    seeded and diced

1 tbsp chopped fresh cilantro

salt and pepper

NEAPOLITAN SEAFOOD SALAD

SERVES 4

1 lb/450 g prepared squid,
   cut into strips

1 lb 10 oz/750 g cooked mussels

1 lb 10 oz/750 g cooked
   cockles in brine

scant ¾ cup white wine

1½ cups olive oil

2 cups dried pasta shapes,
   such as campanelle

juice of 1 lemon

1 bunch chives, snipped

1 bunch fresh flat-leaf parsley,
   finely chopped

handful of mixed salad greens

salt and pepper

4 large tomatoes, to garnish

Put all of the seafood into a large bowl. Pour over the wine and half the olive oil, then set aside for 6 hours.

Put the seafood mixture into a pan and simmer over a low heat for 10 minutes. Set aside to cool.

Bring a large pan of lightly salted water to a boil. Add the pasta and 1 tbsp of the remaining olive oil and cook for 10–12 minutes, until just tender. Drain thoroughly and refresh in cold water.

Strain off about half of the cooking liquid from the seafood and discard the rest. Mix in the lemon juice, chives, parsley, and the remaining olive oil. Season to taste with salt and pepper. Drain the pasta and add to the seafood.

Shred the salad greens and arrange them at the bottom of a salad bowl. Cut the tomatoes into quarters. Spoon the seafood salad into the bowl, garnish with the tomatoes, and serve.

VEGETARIAN

TRADITIONAL
GREEK SALAD

To make the dressing, whisk the dressing ingredients together in a bowl. Cut the feta cheese into cubes about 1 inch/2.5 cm square. Put the lettuce, tomatoes, and cucumber in a salad bowl. Scatter over the cheese and toss together.

Just before serving, whisk the dressing, pour over the salad greens, and toss together. Scatter over the olives and chopped herbs and serve.

SERVES 4

7 oz/200 g Greek feta cheese

½ head iceberg lettuce, or 1 lettuce such as romaine or escarole, shredded or sliced

4 tomatoes, cut into quarters

½ cucumber, sliced

12 Greek black olives, pitted

2 tbsp chopped fresh herbs, such as oregano, flat-leaf parsley, mint, or basil

dressing

6 tbsp extra virgin olive oil

2 tbsp fresh lemon juice

1 garlic clove, crushed

pinch of sugar

salt and pepper

ROASTED VEGETABLE SALAD

Preheat the oven to 400°F/200°C. Cut all the vegetables into even-size wedges, put into a roasting pan, and sprinkle over the garlic.

Pour over 2 tablespoons of the olive oil and turn the vegetables in the oil until well coated. Add a little salt and pepper. Roast in the preheated oven for 40 minutes, or until tender, adding the extra olive oil if becoming too dry.

To make the dressing, place the ingredients in a screw-top jar and shake vigorously until they are well blended.

Once the vegetables are cooked, remove from the oven, arrange on a serving dish, and pour over the dressing. Sprinkle with the basil. Serve with Parmesan cheese and fresh crusty bread.

SERVES 4

1 onion

1 eggplant, about 8 oz/225 g

1 red bell pepper, seeded

1 orange bell pepper, seeded

1 large zucchini, about 6 oz/175 g

2–4 garlic cloves

2–4 tbsp olive oil

1 tbsp shredded fresh basil

salt and pepper

freshly shaved Parmesan cheese and fresh crusty bread, to serve

dressing

1 tbsp balsamic vinegar

2 tbsp extra virgin olive oil

TUSCAN BREAD SALAD

SERVES 4

1 small stale ciabatta loaf

2–3 tbsp cold water

6 large ripe plum tomatoes

¼ cucumber, peeled and coarsely
  chopped

1 small red onion, very thinly
  sliced

handful fresh basil leaves

dressing

4 tbsp extra virgin olive oil,
  plus extra for drizzling

1 tbsp red wine vinegar

pinch of sugar

2 tsp capers, drained and rinsed

salt and pepper

Tear the bread into bite-size chunks and put them into a large shallow dish. Sprinkle with the water. Coarsely chop 3 of the tomatoes and add to the dish with the cucumber and onion. Stir to mix. Tear half the basil leaves and sprinkle them over the top.

Halve the remaining tomatoes and squeeze each half to extract as much of the juice and seeds as possible into a small bowl. Discard any remaining skin and flesh.

Add the olive oil, vinegar, sugar, and capers to the tomato juice and seeds and whisk together. Season to taste with salt and pepper. Pour the tomato dressing over the bread salad and toss well. Chill in the refrigerator for at least 30 minutes. Serve garnished with the remaining basil leaves and drizzled with a little more olive oil.

TOMATO & MOZZARELLA SALAD

Using a sharp knife, cut the tomatoes into thick wedges and place in a large serving dish. Drain the mozzarella and coarsely tear into pieces. Cut the avocados in half and remove the pits. Cut the flesh into slices, then arrange the mozzarella and avocado with the tomatoes.

To make the dressing, mix the dressing ingredients together in a separate bowl. Drizzle the dressing over the salad.

Sprinkle the basil and olives over the top, season and serve at once with fresh crusty bread.

SERVES 4

2 ripe beefsteak tomatoes

5½ oz/150 g fresh mozzarella

2 avocados

few fresh basil leaves, torn into
  pieces

20 black olives

salt and pepper

fresh crusty bread, to serve

dressing

4 tbsp olive oil

1½ tbsp white wine vinegar

1 tsp coarse-grain mustard

SUN-DRIED TOMATO SALAD

To make the dressing, put the sun-dried tomatoes, basil, parsley, capers, vinegar, and garlic in a food processor or blender. Measure the oil from the sun-dried tomatoes jar and make it up to ⅔ cup with more olive oil if necessary. Add it to the food processor or blender and process until smooth. Season to taste with pepper.

Divide the salad greens among 4 individual serving plates. Top with the slices of mozzarella and spoon the dressing over them. Serve immediately.

SERVES 4

4 cups mixed salad greens, such as oak leaf lettuce, baby spinach, and arugula

1 lb 2 oz/500 g smoked mozzarella cheese, sliced

dressing

1¼ cups drained sun-dried tomatoes in olive oil, reserving the oil from the jar

¼ cup coarsely shredded fresh basil

¼ cup coarsely chopped fresh flat-leaf parsley

1 tbsp capers, rinsed

1 tbsp balsamic vinegar

1 garlic clove, coarsely chopped

extra olive oil, if necessary

pepper

ASPARAGUS & TOMATO SALAD

SERVES 4

8 oz/225 g asparagus spears

1 handful corn salad

1 handful arugula or mizuna
  leaves

1 lb/450 g ripe tomatoes, sliced

12 black olives, pitted and
  chopped

1 tbsp toasted pine nuts

dressing

1 tsp lemon oil

1 tbsp olive oil

1 tsp whole-grain mustard

2 tbsp balsamic vinegar

salt and pepper

Steam the asparagus spears for 8 minutes, or until tender. Rinse under cold running water to prevent them from cooking any further, then cut into 2-inch/5-cm pieces.

Arrange the corn salad and arugula around a salad platter to form the base of the salad. Place the sliced tomatoes in a circle on top and the asparagus in the center.

Sprinkle the black olives and pine nuts over the top. To make the dressing, place all the ingredients in a screw-top jar and shake vigorously until they are well blended. Drizzle over the salad and serve.

CAULIFLOWER, BROCCOLI & CASHEW NUT SALAD

Heat the oil in a preheated wok. Add the onions and stir-fry over medium–high heat for 3–4 minutes, or until starting to brown. Add the cauliflower and broccoli and stir-fry for 1–2 minutes. Stir in the curry paste and stir-fry for 30 seconds, then add the coconut milk, jaggery, and salt. Bring gently to a boil, stirring occasionally, then reduce the heat and simmer gently for 3–4 minutes, or until the vegetables are almost tender.

Meanwhile, heat a separate dry skillet until hot. Add the cashew nuts and cook, shaking the skillet frequently, for 2–3 minutes, or until lightly browned. Add to the stir-fry with the cilantro and stir well, then serve immediately, garnished with torn sprigs of cilantro.

SERVES 4

2 tbsp peanut oil or vegetable oil

2 red onions, cut into wedges

1 small head cauliflower, cut into florets

1 small head broccoli, cut into florets

2 tbsp prepared yellow curry paste or red curry paste

1 ¾ cups canned coconut milk

1 tsp jaggery or light brown sugar

1 tsp salt

½ cup unsalted cashew nuts

handful of fresh cilantro, chopped, plus extra sprigs, torn, to garnish

NEW POTATO & RADISH SALAD

Cook the potatoes in a large pan of lightly salted boiling water for 12–15 minutes, until tender. Drain well and let cool. Transfer to a serving bowl and stir in the radishes.

To make the dressing, put the sour cream and milk into a bowl and whisk until smooth. Stir in the cornichons and dill and season to taste with salt and pepper.

Pour the dressing over the potatoes and radishes and toss to coat. Add the red onion and arugula leaves and mix gently.

SERVES 4

1 lb 2 oz/500 g new potatoes, halved

8 radishes, thinly sliced

1 small red onion, thinly sliced

1¼ cups wild arugula leaves

dressing

⅔ cup sour cream

2 tbsp milk

3 cornichons (small dill pickles), drained and finely chopped

2 tbsp chopped fresh dill

salt and pepper

WARM NEW POTATO & LENTIL SALAD

SERVES 4

³⁄₈ cup Puy lentils

1 lb/450 g new potatoes

6 scallions

1 tbsp olive oil

2 tbsp balsamic vinegar

salt and pepper

Bring a large pan of water to a boil. Rinse the lentils, then cook for 20 minutes, or until tender. Drain and rinse, then put to one side.

Meanwhile, steam or boil the potatoes until they are soft all the way through. Drain and halve.

Trim the bottom from the scallions and cut them in long strips.

Put the lentils, potatoes, and scallions into a serving dish and toss with the olive oil and vinegar. Season with plenty of pepper and a little salt if required.

SWEET POTATO SALAD

Preheat the oven to 375°F/190°C. Put the sweet potato chunks into a roasting pan with the oil, pepper to taste, and garlic and toss to combine. Roast in the preheated oven for 30 minutes, or until soft and slightly charred.

Meanwhile, preheat the broiler to high. Arrange the eggplant and bell pepper slices on the broiler pan and cook under the preheated broiler, turning occasionally, for 10 minutes, or until soft and slightly charred.

To make the dressing, whisk the vinegar, garlic, and oil together in a small bowl and stir in the shallot and herbs. Season to taste with pepper.

To serve, divide the salad greens among 4 serving plates and arrange the sweet potato, eggplant, bell peppers, and mozzarella on top. Drizzle with the dressing and serve.

SERVES 4

2 sweet potatoes, peeled and cut into chunks

2 tbsp olive oil

2 garlic cloves, crushed

1 large eggplant, sliced

2 red bell peppers, seeded and sliced

7 oz/200 g package mixed salad greens

11 oz/300 g mozzarella cheese, drained and sliced

pepper

dressing

1 tbsp balsamic vinegar

1 garlic clove, crushed

3 tbsp olive oil

1 small shallot, finely chopped

2 tbsp chopped mixed fresh herbs, such as tarragon, chervil, and basil

SWEET POTATO & BEAN SALAD

Bring a pan of water to a boil over medium heat. Add the sweet potato and cook for 10 minutes, until tender. Drain the potato, transfer to a bowl, and set aside.

Cook the carrots in a separate pan of boiling water for 1 minute. Drain thoroughly and add to the sweet potato. Cut the tops off the tomatoes and scoop out the seeds. Chop the flesh and add to the bowl with the celery and beans. Mix well.

Line a large serving bowl with the mixed salad greens. Spoon the sweet potato-and-bean mixture on top, then sprinkle with the golden raisins and scallions.

To make the dressing, place all the ingredients in a screw-top jar and shake vigorously until they are well blended. Pour over the salad and serve.

SERVES 4

1 sweet potato, peeled and diced

4 baby carrots, halved

4 tomatoes

4 celery stalks, chopped

8 oz/225 g canned cranberry beans, drained and rinsed

4 cups mixed salad greens, such as frisée, arugula, radicchio, and oak leaf lettuce

1 tbsp golden raisins

4 scallions, sliced diagonally

dressing

2 tbsp lemon juice

1 garlic clove, crushed

⅔ cup plain yogurt

2 tbsp olive oil

salt and pepper

GREEN BEAN SALAD WITH FETA

SERVES 4

12 oz/350 g green beans, trimmed

1 red onion, chopped

3–4 tbsp chopped fresh cilantro

2 radishes, thinly sliced

¾ cup crumbled feta cheese

1 tsp chopped fresh oregano or
 ½ tsp dried oregano

2 tbsp red wine vinegar or fruit
 vinegar

5 tbsp extra virgin olive oil

3 ripe tomatoes (optional),
 cut into wedges

pepper

Bring about 2 inches/5 cm water to a boil in the bottom of a steamer or in a medium saucepan. Add the green beans to the top of the steamer or place them in a metal colander set over the saucepan of water. Cover and steam the beans for about 5 minutes, until just tender.

Transfer the beans to a bowl and add the onion, cilantro, radishes, crumbled feta cheese, and oregano.

Grind pepper over to taste. Whisk the vinegar and olive oil together and then pour over the salad. Toss gently to mix well.

Transfer to a serving platter, surround with the tomato wedges, if using, and serve at once or chill until ready to serve.

GREEN BEAN & WALNUT SALAD

Cook the beans for 3–4 minutes. Drain well, refresh under cold running water, and drain again. Put into a mixing bowl and add the onion, garlic, and cheese.

To make the dressing, place all the ingredients in a screw-top jar and shake vigorously until they are well blended. Pour the dressing over the salad and toss gently to coat. Cover with plastic wrap and chill for at least 30 minutes. Remove the beans from the refrigerator 10 minutes before serving. Give them a quick stir and transfer to serving dishes.

Toast the nuts in a dry skillet over medium heat for 2 minutes, or until they begin to brown. Sprinkle the toasted nuts over the beans to garnish before serving and serve with extra Parmesan cheese.

SERVES 2

1 lb/450 g green beans, trimmed and halved

1 small onion, finely chopped

1 garlic clove, chopped

4 tbsp freshly grated Parmesan cheese, plus extra to serve

chopped walnuts or almonds, to garnish

dressing

6 tbsp olive oil

2 tbsp white wine vinegar

2 tsp chopped fresh tarragon

salt and pepper

HERBED MIXED BEAN SALAD

To make the dressing, place all the ingredients in a screw-top jar and shake vigorously until they are well blended.

Prepare a bowl of iced water. Bring a pan of lightly salted water to a boil. Add the green beans and fava beans and blanch for 3 minutes, or until just tender. Remove the beans from the water and immediately transfer them to the iced water.

Return the water to a boil and blanch the peas for 3 minutes, or until tender. Remove from the water and add to the iced water to cool. Drain the beans and peas and pat dry with paper towels. Transfer to a large bowl, add the dressing, cannellini beans, onion, and herbs and toss. Cover and chill.

To make the cheese, just before you are ready to serve, heat a thin layer of oil in a large skillet over medium–high heat. Lightly dust each slice of cheese with flour, shaking off the excess. Place as many pieces as will fit in the skillet and fry for 30–60 seconds, until golden brown. Flip the cheese over and continue frying until lightly browned on the other side, then remove from the skillet and keep warm while you fry the remaining pieces.

Toss the salad again, add the arugula leaves, and then add extra seasoning, if necessary. Divide the salad among individual plates and arrange the hot cheese alongside.

SERVES 4–6

1 cup green beans, trimmed and halved

¾ cup shelled fava beans

¾ cup fresh peas

14 oz/400 g canned cannellini beans, drained and rinsed

1 small red onion, thinly sliced

2 tbsp chopped fresh parsley

1 tbsp snipped fresh chives

4½ cups arugula leaves

salt and pepper

dressing

5 tbsp extra virgin olive oil

2 tbsp tarragon vinegar

½ tsp mixed-grain mustard

pinch of sugar

fried provolone cheese

olive oil

12 oz/350 g provolone cheese, cut into 12 slices

all-purpose flour, for dusting

PASTA SALAD WITH BELL PEPPERS

SERVES 4

1 red bell pepper

1 orange bell pepper

10 oz/280 g dried pasta shells,
   such as conchiglie

5 tbsp extra virgin olive oil

2 tbsp lemon juice

2 tbsp green pesto

1 garlic clove, finely chopped

3 tbsp shredded fresh basil leaves

salt and pepper

Preheat the broiler. Put the whole bell peppers on a baking sheet and place under the hot broiler, turning frequently, for 15 minutes, or until charred all over. Remove with tongs and place in a bowl. Cover with crumpled paper towels and reserve.

Meanwhile, bring a large saucepan of lightly salted water to a boil. Add the pasta, return to a boil, and cook for 8–10 minutes until tender, or according to package directions.

Combine the olive oil, lemon juice, pesto, and garlic in a bowl, whisking well to mix. Drain the pasta, add it to the pesto mixture while still hot, and toss well. Reserve.

When the bell peppers are cool enough to handle, peel off the skins, then cut open and remove the seeds. Chop the flesh coarsely and add to the pasta with the basil. Season to taste with salt and pepper and toss well. Serve.

VEGETARIAN

199

MARINATED BELL PEPPER SALAD

Preheat the oven to 375°F/190°C. Halve the bell peppers, keeping the stalks on. Remove the white seeds and pith. Put the bell peppers, cut side uppermost, into a shallow roasting pan. Sprinkle with the onion and garlic, season with salt and pepper, and drizzle with half the olive oil. Roast for 40 minutes, until the bell peppers are tender. Let cool.

Put the cold bell peppers on a serving plate and pour any juices left in the roasting pan over them. Sprinkle with the olives, mozzarella balls, and basil.

Whisk together the remaining olive oil and the balsamic vinegar and pour the mixture over the bell peppers. Cover and let marinate in the refrigerator for at least 2 hours (or overnight) before serving.

SERVES 4

2 red bell peppers

2 yellow bell peppers

1 red onion, coarsely chopped

2 garlic cloves, chopped

6 tbsp olive oil

1 cup drained marinated black olives

3½ oz/100 g mini mozzarella balls, drained

2 tbsp coarsely torn fresh basil leaves

2 tbsp balsamic vinegar

salt and pepper

WILD RICE SALAD

Put the wild rice and water into a large pan and bring to a boil. Stir, then cover and simmer for 40 minutes, or until the rice is firm to the bite. Uncover the rice for the last few minutes of cooking to let any excess water evaporate.

To make the dressing, place all the ingredients in a screw-top jar and shake vigorously until they are well blended.

Drain the rice and turn into a large bowl. Pour over the dressing and mix in. Then mix in the chopped bell peppers, cucumber, orange, tomatoes, red onion, and flat-leaf parsley and serve.

SERVES 4

1⅓ cups wild rice

3½ cups water

1 each red, yellow, and orange bell peppers, skinned, seeded, and thinly sliced

½ cucumber, halved lengthwise and sliced

1 orange, peeled, pith removed, and cubed

3 ripe tomatoes, cut into chunks

1 red onion, finely chopped

generous handful chopped fresh flat-leaf parsley

dressing

1 clove garlic, crushed

1 tbsp balsamic vinegar

2 tbsp extra virgin olive oil

salt and pepper

SPICED ORANGE & CARROT SALAD

SERVES 4

3²⁄₃ cups coarsely grated carrots

4 scallions, finely shredded

2 oranges

generous ¹⁄₃ cup raisins

3 tbsp chopped fresh cilantro

fresh cilantro sprigs, to garnish
  (optional)

dressing

3 tbsp olive oil

3 tbsp orange juice

2 tsp lemon juice

½ tsp ground cumin

½ tsp ground coriander

salt and pepper

Put the carrots and scallions into a large bowl and toss gently to mix. Using a serrated knife, remove all the peel and pith from the oranges, then cut into segments between the membranes. Gently toss the orange segments into the bowl with the raisins and chopped cilantro.

To make the dressing, mix the dressing ingredients together in a separate bowl.

Pour the dressing over the carrot salad and toss thoroughly. Cover with plastic wrap and chill in the refrigerator for 30 minutes. Adjust the seasoning to taste. Serve garnished with fresh cilantro sprigs, if using.

WARM RED LENTIL SALAD

Heat half the olive oil in a large pan over medium heat, add the cumin seeds, garlic, and ginger and cook for 2 minutes, stirring constantly.

Stir in the lentils, then add the stock, a ladleful at a time, until it is all absorbed, stirring constantly—this will take about 20 minutes. Remove from the heat and stir in the herbs.

Meanwhile, heat the remaining olive oil in a skillet over medium heat, add the onions, and cook, stirring frequently, for 10 minutes, or until soft and lightly browned.

Toss the spinach in the hazelnut oil in a bowl, then divide among 4 serving plates.

Mash the goat cheese with the yogurt in a small bowl and season to taste with pepper.

Divide the lentils among the serving plates and top with the onions and goat cheese mixture.

SERVES 4

2 tbsp olive oil

2 tsp cumin seeds

2 garlic cloves, crushed

2 tsp grated fresh ginger

1½ cups split red lentils

3 cups vegetable stock

2 tbsp chopped fresh mint

2 tbsp chopped fresh cilantro

2 red onions, thinly sliced

4½ cups baby spinach leaves

1 tsp hazelnut oil

5½ oz/150 g soft goat cheese

4 tbsp strained plain yogurt

pepper

GOAT CHEESE CROUTON & SPINACH SALAD

Preheat the broiler to medium. To make the dressing, place all the ingredients in a screw-top jar and shake vigorously until they are well blended.

Lightly brush the slices of French bread with olive oil. Toast the slices under the broiler for 1–2 minutes on each side, until just golden. Top each with a slice of goat cheese, season with pepper, and broil for another 1–2 minutes, until the cheese has melted.

Meanwhile, put the spinach into a large bowl. Add nearly all the dressing and toss gently to coat the leaves. Divide between 2 serving plates. Add the sun-blush tomatoes and top with the cheese croutons. Drizzle with the rest of the dressing and serve immediately.

SERVES 2

6 thin slices French bread

1 tbsp olive oil

4 oz/115 g round goat cheese (with rind), cut into 6 slices

3 cups baby spinach leaves

½ cup drained sun-blush or sun-dried tomatoes

dressing

3 tbsp extra virgin olive oil

1 tbsp sherry vinegar

1 tsp whole-grain mustard

pinch of sugar

salt and pepper

CHILI SPICED PANEER SALAD

SERVES 2

6 tbsp sunflower oil

8 oz/225 g paneer, cubed

1 tsp mustard seeds

1 tsp ground cumin

1 garlic clove, crushed

1 small green chile, seeded and finely chopped

3 cups scallions, finely chopped

3 oz/85 g baby salad greens

tomato chutney

2 ripe tomatoes, peeled, seeded, and diced

1 shallot, finely chopped

2 tbsp sunflower oil

2 tsp lemon juice

1 tbsp chopped fresh cilantro

salt and pepper

To make the tomato chutney, mix the ingredients together in a bowl. Chill in the refrigerator for 30 minutes.

Heat the oil in a large skillet. Add the paneer cubes and cook over medium–high heat, turning frequently, for 4–5 minutes, until golden brown all over (be careful because the oil may spit). Remove the paneer with a slotted spoon and drain on paper towels.

Carefully pour off half the hot oil from the skillet. Add the mustard seeds and ground cumin to the remaining oil and fry for a few seconds. Stir in the garlic, chile, and scallions and cook for 1–2 minutes. Return the paneer to the skillet and toss to coat well in the spicy mixture.

Divide the salad greens between 2 serving plates. Top with the hot paneer. Spoon the tomato chutney over it and serve immediately.

BUCKWHEAT NOODLE SALAD

Cook the noodles in a large pan of lightly salted boiling water according to the package instructions. Drain and refresh under cold running water.

To make the dressing, blend the ingredients in a bowl until smooth and creamy.

Place the smoked tofu in a steamer. Steam for 5 minutes, then cut into thin slices.

Meanwhile, put the cabbage, carrots, scallions, and chile into a bowl and toss to mix. To serve, arrange the noodles on serving plates and top with the carrot salad and slices of tofu. Spoon over the dressing and sprinkle with sesame seeds.

SERVES 2

7 oz/200 g buckwheat noodles

9 oz/250 g drained, firm smoked tofu

2¼ cups finely shredded white cabbage

2¼ cups finely shredded carrots

3 scallions, diagonally sliced

1 fresh red chile, seeded and finely sliced into circles

2 tbsp sesame seeds, lightly toasted

dressing

1 tsp grated fresh ginger

1 garlic clove, crushed

6 oz/175 g drained silken tofu

4 tsp tamari (wheat-free soy sauce)

2 tbsp sesame oil

4 tbsp hot water

salt

RED CABBAGE & BEET SLAW

Put the cabbage, beet, and apple slices into a large bowl. Add the lemon juice and mix well.

To make the dressing, mix the dressing ingredients together in a separate bowl. Pour the dressing over the salad and stir well. Season with salt and pepper, cover, and chill in the refrigerator for at least 1 hour.

Stir the salad thoroughly and adjust the seasoning to taste. Sprinkle with the sunflower and pumpkin seeds just before serving.

SERVES 4

3¾ cups finely shredded red cabbage

1 cup julienned cooked beet

1 apple, cored and thinly sliced

1 tbsp lemon juice

1 tbsp sunflower seeds

1 tbsp pumpkin seeds

dressing

3 tbsp mayonnaise

2 tbsp strained plain yogurt

1 tbsp red wine vinegar

salt and pepper

HEALTH-BOOSTING

GREEK FETA
SALAD

To make the dressing, place all the ingredients in a screw-top jar and shake vigorously until they are well blended.

Arrange the grape leaves on a serving dish and then the tomatoes, cucumber, and onion. Sprinkle the cheese and olives on top. Pour the dressing over the salad and serve.

SERVES 4

a few grape leaves

4 tomatoes, sliced

½ cucumber, peeled and sliced

1 small red onion, sliced thinly

4 oz/115 g feta cheese, cubed

8 black olives

dressing

3 tbsp extra virgin olive oil

1 tbsp lemon juice

½ tsp dried oregano

salt and pepper

SALAD WITH GARLIC DRESSING

Gently mix the cucumber batons, scallions, tomato wedges, yellow bell pepper strips, celery strips, radishes, and arugula in a large serving bowl.

To make the dressing, mix the dressing ingredients together in a separate bowl.

Spoon the dressing over the salad and toss to mix. Sprinkle the salad with chopped mint, if using, and serve.

SERVES 4

½ small cucmber, cut into batons

6 scallions, halved

2 tomatoes, seeded and
   cut into 8 wedges

1 yellow bell pepper, seeded and
   cut into strips

2 celery stalks, cut into strips

4 radishes, quartered

4½ cups arugula

chopped fresh mint, to garnish
   (optional)

dressing

2 tbsp lemon juice

1 garlic clove, crushed

⅔ cup plain yogurt

2 tbsp olive oil

salt and pepper

NUTTY BEET
SALAD

SERVES 4

3 tbsp red wine vinegar or fruit
   vinegar

3 cooked beets, grated

2 tart apples

2 tbsp lemon juice

4 large handfuls mixed salad
   greens, to serve

4 tbsp pecans, to garnish

dressing

¼ cup plain yogurt

¼ cup mayonnaise

1 garlic clove, chopped

1 tbsp chopped fresh dill

salt and pepper

Sprinkle vinegar over the beets, cover with plastic wrap, and chill
for at least 4 hours.

Core and slice the apples, place the slices in a dish, and
sprinkle with the lemon juice to prevent discoloration.

To make the dressing, mix the dressing ingredients together
in a separate bowl. Remove the beets from the refrigerator and
dress. Add the apples to the beets and mix gently to coat with
the salad dressing.

To serve, arrange a handful of salad greens on each plate and
top with a large spoonful of the apple-and-beet mixture.

Toast the pecans in a heavy, dry skillet over medium heat for
2 minutes, or until they begin to brown. Sprinkle them over the
beets and apple to garnish.

BULGUR WHEAT
SALAD

Preheat the oven to 400°F/200°C. Put the halved tomatoes into a roasting pan, cut side uppermost. Sprinkle with the garlic, sugar, and sea salt and drizzle with 2 tablespoons of the olive oil. Roast in the oven for 20 minutes, until soft. Let cool.

Put the bulgur wheat into a heatproof bowl and pour in enough boiling water to cover the grains. Cover the bowl and let stand for 30 minutes, until all the liquid has been absorbed. Pour in the vinegar and remaining olive oil and stir thoroughly with a fork. Season well with salt and pepper.

Stir the cucumber, chopped herbs, and pine nuts into the bulgur. Gently stir in the roasted tomatoes and any juices from the roasting pan. Chill in the refrigerator for 30 minutes. Adjust the seasoning to taste and serve garnished with parsley sprigs.

SERVES 4

4 small, vine-ripened tomatoes, halved

2 garlic cloves, finely chopped

1 tsp sugar

1 tsp sea salt flakes

4 tbsp extra virgin olive oil

generous 1 cup bulgur wheat

2 tbsp white wine vinegar

¾ cup peeled and diced cucumber

2 tbsp chopped fresh flat-leaf parsley

2 tbsp chopped fresh mint

2 tbsp pine nuts, lightly toasted

salt and pepper

fresh flat-leaf parsley sprigs, to garnish

TABBOULEH

Put the quinoa into a medium-size pan and cover with the water. Bring to a boil, then reduce the heat, cover, and let simmer over low heat for 15 minutes. Drain if necessary.

Let the quinoa cool slightly before combining with the remaining ingredients in a salad bowl. Adjust the seasoning, if necessary, before serving.

SERVES 4

generous 1 cup quinoa

2½ cups water

10 vine-ripened cherry tomatoes, seeded and halved

3-inch/7.5-cm piece cucumber, diced

3 scallions, finely chopped

juice of ½ lemon

2 tbsp extra virgin olive oil

4 tbsp chopped fresh mint

4 tbsp chopped fresh cilantro

4 tbsp chopped fresh parsley

salt and pepper

QUINOA SALAD WITH SUN-DRIED TOMATOES

SERVES 4

1 cup quinoa

2 cups water

10 sun-dried tomatoes
  (in oil, drained)

½ cup feta cheese, crumbled

2 scallions, white part, chopped

⅓ cup mixed fresh herbs (basil,
  parsley, cilantro), chopped

¼ cup pitted black olives,
  chopped

dressing

⅓ cup roasted tomato oil

3 tbsp fresh lemon juice

1 clove garlic, crushed

salt and pepper

Put the quinoa into a medium-size pan and cover with the water.
Bring to a boil, then reduce the heat, cover, and let simmer over
low heat for 15 minutes. Drain if necessary.

Let the quinoa cool slightly before combining with the
remaining ingredients in a bowl.

To make the dressing, whisk the dressing ingredients together
in a separate bowl. Pour over the quinoa and serve.

SUCCATASH SALAD

Beat the vinegar, mustard, and sugar together. Gradually whisk in the olive and sunflower oils to form an emulsion.

Stir in the corn kernels, green beans, bell peppers, and scallions. Add salt and pepper to taste and stir together again. Cover and chill for up to 1 day until required.

When ready to serve, adjust the seasoning, if necessary, and garnish with parsley.

SERVES 4–6

1 tbsp apple-cider vinegar

1 tsp whole-grain mustard

1 tsp sugar

3 tbsp garlic-flavored olive oil

1 tbsp sunflower oil

14 oz/400 g canned corn kernels, rinsed and drained

14 oz/400 g green beans, finely chopped

2 peeled red bell peppers from a jar, drained and finely chopped

2 scallions, very finely chopped

salt and pepper

fresh flat-leaf parsley sprigs, to garnish

BELL PEPPER & RADICCHIO SALAD

Cut the bell peppers into rounds.

Arrange the radicchio leaves in a salad bowl. Add the bell pepper, beets, radishes, and scallions. Drizzle with the vinaigrette and serve with crusty bread.

SERVES 4

2 red bell peppers, cored and seeded

1 head radicchio, separated into leaves

4 cooked whole beets, cut into matchsticks

12 radishes, sliced

4 scallions, finely chopped

4 tbsp vinaigrette

fresh crusty bread, to serve

WATERCRESS, ZUCCHINI & MINT SALAD

SERVES 4

2 zucchini, cut into batons

1 cup chopped green beans

1 green bell pepper, seeded
   and cut into strips

2 celery stalks, sliced

1 bunch watercress

salt

dressing

scant 1 cup plain yogurt

1 garlic clove, crushed

2 tbsp chopped fresh mint pepper

Bring a saucepan of lightly salted water to a boil, add the
zucchini batons and green beans, and cook for 7–8 minutes.
Drain, rinse under cold running water, and drain again. Set aside
to cool completely.

Mix the zucchini and green beans with the bell pepper strips,
celery, and watercress in a large serving bowl.

To make the dressing, mix the dressing ingredients together in
a separate bowl.

Spoon the dressing onto the salad and serve immediately.

CHICKPEA & TOMATO SALAD

If using dried chickpeas, soak overnight, then boil for 30 minutes, or until soft. Let cool.

To make the dressing, place all the ingredients in a screw-top jar and shake vigorously until they are well blended. Taste and add more lemon juice or oil if necessary.

Add the tomatoes, onion, and basil to the chickpeas and mix gently. Pour over the dressing and mix again. Arrange on a bed of lettuce and serve with crusty bread.

SERVES 4

scant 1 cup dried chickpeas

2–3 ripe tomatoes, coarsely chopped

1 red onion, thinly sliced

handful fresh basil leaves, torn

1 romaine lettuce, torn

fresh crusty bread, to serve

dressing

1 green chile, seeded and finely chopped

1 garlic clove, crushed

juice and zest of 2 lemons

2 tbsp olive oil

1 tbsp water

pepper

MINTED PEA & GREEN BEAN RICE SALAD

To make the dressing, whisk the dressing ingredients together in a bowl.

Cook the rice in a pan of lightly salted boiling water for 10–12 minutes, or until just tender. Drain well and transfer to a large serving bowl. Stir in the dressing and let cool.

Cook the green beans, snow peas, and peas in a pan of boiling water for 2 minutes. Drain well and refresh under cold running water. Stir into the rice. Adjust the seasoning to taste and serve garnished with the mint leaves.

SERVES 6

scant 1 cup easy-cook, long grain rice

1 cup trimmed and diagonally sliced green beans

1 cup snow peas, thinly sliced

1 cup frozen peas

few fresh mint leaves, to garnish

dressing

4 scallions, finely chopped

4 tbsp sunflower oil

2 tbsp white wine vinegar

½ tsp Dijon mustard

2 tbsp finely chopped fresh mint

salt and pepper

THREE BEAN SALAD

SERVES 4–6

6 oz/175 g package mixed salad greens, such as spinach, arugula, and frisée

1 red onion

¾ cup sliced radishes

10 cherry tomatoes, halved

4 oz/115 g cooked beet, diced

10 oz/280 g canned cannellini beans, drained and rinsed

7 oz/200 g canned red kidney beans, drained and rinsed

10½ oz/300 g canned flageolets, drained and rinsed

scant ⅓ cup dried cranberries

scant ½ cup roasted cashews

1½ cups crumbled feta cheese

dressing

4 tbsp extra virgin olive oil

1 tsp Dijon mustard

2 tbsp lemon juice

1 tbsp chopped fresh cilantro

salt and pepper

Arrange the salad greens in a salad bowl and set aside.

Thinly slice the onion, then cut in half to form half moons and put into a bowl.

To make the dressing, place all the ingredients in a screw-top jar and shake vigorously until they are well blended. Add to the onion with the remaining ingredients, except the nuts and cheese. Pour over the beans, toss lightly, then spoon on top of the salad greens.

Sprinkle over the nuts and cheese and serve at once.

241

SOYBEAN & MUSHROOM SALAD

Steam the soybeans in a steamer or metal colander set over a pan of simmering water for 5–6 minutes, until just tender. Rinse with cold water, drain well, and transfer to a serving bowl. Add the mushrooms, spinach, and arugula leaves and gently toss together.

To make the dressing, whisk the dressing ingredients together in a separate bowl. Pour the dressing over the salad and toss well to mix. Serve immediately with extra pepper.

SERVES 2

¾ cup fresh soybeans (edamame)

scant 1 cup sliced closed-cup mushrooms

2 cups baby spinach leaves

handful of wild arugula leaves

dressing

3 tbsp light olive oil

1½ tbsp lemon juice

½ tsp Dijon mustard

1 tbsp snipped fresh chives

1 tbsp chopped fresh parsley

salt and pepper

FRUITY COTTAGE CHEESE SALAD

Place the cottage cheese in a bowl and stir in the chopped herbs. Cover lightly and set aside.

Cut the peeled bell peppers into thin strips and set aside. Cut the melon in half, discard the seeds and cut into small wedges. Remove and discard the rind, or run a sharp knife between the skin and flesh to loosen, then cut the flesh horizontally across. Push the flesh in alternate directions but so that it still sits on the skin. Set aside.

Arrange the salad greens on a large serving platter with the melon wedges.

Spoon the herb-flavored cottage cheese on the platter and arrange the reserved bell peppers, the grapes, and red onion slices around the cheese.

To make the dressing, mix the dressing ingredients together in a separate bowl. Drizzle over the salad and serve.

SERVES 4

⅓ cup cottage cheese

1 tsp chopped fresh parsley

1 tbsp snipped fresh chives

1 tsp chopped fresh chervil or basil

2 assorted colored bell peppers, seeded, roasted, and peeled

1 small melon, such as ogen or other cantaloupe

6 oz/175 g assorted salad greens

½ cup seedless grapes

1 red onion, thinly sliced

dressing

3 tbsp freshly squeezed lime juice

1 small fresh red chile, seeded and finely chopped

1 tsp honey

1 tbsp soy sauce

INDONESIAN WARM SALAD

SERVES 4

8 outer leaves romaine lettuce

1 cup halved and lightly cooked
   green beans

½ cup lightly cooked baby carrots

9 oz/250 g new potatoes, cooked
   until just tender

1 tbsp peanut oil

generous ¾ cup fresh bean
   sprouts

3¼-inch/8-cm piece cucumber,
   seeded and cut into 1½-inch/
   4-cm batons

4 eggs, hard-cooked

1 small mild onion, sliced into
   rings

sauce

4 tbsp canned reduced-fat coconut
   milk

3 tbsp sugar-free smooth peanut
   butter

juice of ½ lime

2 tsp light soy sauce

dash of Tabasco sauce or any chili
   sauce

Roughly tear the lettuce leaves, if large, and arrange on
4 individual serving plates. Arrange the green beans and carrots
with the potatoes (cut into chunks if large) on the plates or platter.

   Heat the oil in a nonstick skillet or wok over high heat, then
add the bean sprouts and stir-fry for 2 minutes, or until lightly
cooked or still crisp. Remove with a slotted spoon and sprinkle
over the cooked vegetables with the cucumber. Peel and quarter
the eggs, then arrange on top of the salad.

   Add the onion rings to the oil remaining in the skillet or
wok and stir-fry over high heat for 5 minutes, or until golden
and crisp. Combine all the ingredients for the sauce in a small
bowl and pour over the salad. Top with the onion rings and
serve immediately.

VEGETABLE & RICE NOODLE SALAD

To make the dressing, whisk the dressing ingredients together in a bowl. Put the noodles into a shallow bowl, pour boiling water over them, and let soak for 5 minutes. Drain well and refresh under cold running water. Transfer to a salad bowl, pour half the salad dressing over them, and toss well.

Heat the sesame oil in a wok and stir-fry the garlic and ginger for 1 minute. Add the corn, broccoli, snow peas, and bell pepper and stir-fry over high heat for 2–3 minutes.

Add the hot vegetables to the noodles with the rest of the salad dressing and toss together. Cool, then stir in the bean sprouts. Serve piled into individual bowls garnished with cilantro leaves and chopped chile.

SERVES 2

4½ oz/125 g rice noodles

2 tsp toasted sesame oil

1 garlic clove, crushed

1 tsp grated fresh ginger

1 cup baby corn, thinly sliced

¾ cup tiny broccoli florets

½ cup thinly sliced snow peas

½ red bell pepper, seeded and thinly sliced

1½ cups bean sprouts

fresh cilantro leaves and chopped fresh red chile, to garnish

dressing

2 tbsp peanut oil

1½ tbsp lime juice

2 tbsp sweet chili sauce

salt and pepper

WARM ORIENTAL-STYLE SALAD

Cut the broccoli into tiny florets, then bring a small pan of water to a boil and add the halved carrots. Cook for 3 minutes then add the broccoli and cook for another 2 minutes. Drain and plunge into cold water, then drain again, and set aside.

Arrange 2 bok choy leaves on a large serving platter. Shred the remainder and set aside.

Heat a wok and when hot, add the oil and heat for 30 seconds. Add the sliced onion, chiles, ginger, and star anise and stir-fry for 1 minute. Add the bell pepper strips, zucchini, and baby corn and stir-fry for an additional 2 minutes.

Pour in the orange juice and soy sauce and continue to stir-fry for another 1 minute before adding the reserved shredded bok choy. Stir-fry for 2 minutes, or until the vegetables are tender but still firm to the bite. Arrange the warm salad on the bok choy-lined serving platter, scatter the cashew nuts over the top, and serve.

SERVES 4

1¾ cups small broccoli florets

8 baby carrots, scraped and cut in half lengthwise

10 bok choy leaves

2 sprays sunflower oil

1 red onion, sliced

1–2 fresh Thai chiles, seeded and sliced

1-inch/2.5-cm piece fresh ginger, peeled and grated

2 whole star anise

1 red bell pepper, seeded and cut into strips

1 orange bell pepper, seeded and cut into strips

8 baby zucchini, trimmed and sliced diagonally

1 cup baby corn, sliced in half lengthwise

2 tbsp orange juice

1 tbsp soy sauce

1 tbsp cashew nuts

CHICKEN & SPINACH SALAD

SERVES 4

3 celery stalks, thinly sliced

½ cucumber, thinly sliced

2 scallions, thinly sliced

9 oz/250 g package young
   spinach leaves

3 tbsp chopped fresh parsley

12 oz/350 g cooked boneless
   chicken, sliced thinly

smoked almonds, to garnish
   (optional)

dressing

1-inch/2.5-cm piece of fresh
   ginger, grated finely

3 tbsp olive oil

1 tbsp white wine vinegar

1 tbsp honey

½ tsp ground cinnamon

salt and pepper

Toss the celery, cucumber, and scallions in a large bowl with the spinach leaves and parsley.

Transfer to serving plates and arrange the chicken on top of the salad.

To make the dressing, mix the dressing ingredients together in a separate bowl and pour over the salad. Sprinkle with a few smoked almonds, if using.

THAI-STYLE CHICKEN SALAD

Bring two pans of water to the boil. Put the potatoes into one pan and cook for 15 minutes, until tender. Put the baby corn into the other pan and cook for 5 minutes, until tender. Drain the potatoes and baby corn well and let cool.

When the vegetables are cool, transfer them into a large serving dish. Add the bean sprouts, scallions, chicken, lemongrass, and cilantro and season with salt and pepper.

To make the dressing, place all the ingredients in a screw-top jar and shake vigorously until they are well blended. Drizzle the dressing over the salad and garnish with lime wedges and cilantro leaves. Serve at once.

SERVES 4

14 oz/400 g small new potatoes, scrubbed and cut in half, lengthwise

1 cup baby corn

1½ cups bean sprouts

3 scallions, trimmed and sliced

4 cooked, skinless, boneless chicken breasts, sliced

1 tbsp chopped lemongrass

2 tbsp chopped fresh cilantro

salt and pepper

wedges of lime and fresh cilantro leaves, to garnish

dressing

6 tbsp chili oil or sesame oil

2 tbsp lime juice

1 tbsp light soy sauce

1 tbsp chopped fresh cilantro

1 small red chile, seeded and finely sliced

TURKEY SALAD POCKETS

Preheat the broiler to high.

Put the spinach leaves, bell pepper, carrot, and hummus into a large bowl and stir together, so all the salad ingredients are coated with the hummus. Stir in the turkey and sunflower seeds and season to taste with salt and pepper.

Put the pita under the broiler for about 1 minute on each side to warm through, but do not brown. Cut it in half to make 2 "pockets" of bread.

Divide the salad among the bread pockets and serve.

MAKES 2

small handful baby leaf spinach, rinsed, patted dry, and shredded

½ red bell pepper, seeded and thinly sliced

½ carrot, peeled and coarsely grated

4 tbsp hummus

3 oz/85 g boneless, skinless cooked turkey meat, thinly sliced

½ tbsp toasted sunflower seeds

1 whole wheat pita

salt and pepper

TUNA & AVOCADO SALAD

SERVES 4

2 avocados, pitted, peeled, and cubed

1³/₄ cups halved cherry tomatoes

2 red bell peppers, seeded and chopped

1 bunch fresh flat-leaf parsley, chopped

2 garlic cloves, crushed

1 fresh red chile, seeded and finely chopped

juice of ½ lemon

6 tbsp olive oil

3 tbsp sesame seeds

4 fresh tuna steaks, about 5½ oz/150 g each

8 cooked new potatoes, cubed

arugula leaves and fresh crusty bread, to serve

pepper

Toss the avocados, tomatoes, red bell peppers, parsley, garlic, chile, lemon juice, and 2 tablespoons of the oil together in a large bowl. Season to taste with pepper, cover, and let chill in the refrigerator for 30 minutes.

Lightly crush the sesame seeds in a mortar with a pestle. Tip the crushed seeds onto a plate and spread out. Press each tuna steak in turn into the crushed seeds to coat on both sides.

Heat 2 tablespoons of the remaining oil in a skillet, add the potatoes, and cook, stirring frequently, for 5–8 minutes, or until crisp and brown. Remove from the skillet and drain on paper towels.

Wipe out the skillet, add the remaining oil, and heat over high heat until very hot. Add the tuna steaks and cook for 3–4 minutes on each side.

To serve, divide the avocado salad among 4 serving plates. Top each with a tuna steak, sprinkle over the potatoes and arugula leaves, and serve with crusty bread.

TUNA WITH BEAN SPROUTS SALAD

Combine the soy sauce, oil, and ginger in a shallow dish. Add the tuna steaks and turn to coat in the marinade. Cover and let marinate for 1 hour at room temperature.

Heat a cast-iron grill pan until very hot. Drain the tuna steaks from the marinade and put them into the hot pan. Cook for 2 minutes, then turn over, and cook for 1–2 minutes more, until the steaks are well seared but still a little pink in the middle. Cook for an additional 2–3 minutes if you prefer the tuna well done.

To make the dressing, put all the ingredients into a small pan and heat gently, stirring, until just warmed through.

Combine the alfalfa sprouts, lentil sprouts, and mustard and cress in a bowl and toss with the lime juice. Season with salt and pepper.

Divide the sprout mixture among 4 serving plates and top with the tuna steaks. Drizzle the warm dressing over them.

Garnish with lime wedges and serve immediately.

SERVES 4

2 tbsp soy sauce

1 tbsp sunflower oil

1 tsp grated fresh ginger

4 tuna steaks, about
 6 oz/175 g each

1 cup alfalfa sprouts

1 cup lentil or bean sprouts

½ cup mixed cress, such as
 mustard and garden cress

squeeze of lime or lemon juice

salt and pepper

lime wedges, to garnish

dressing

3 tbsp sunflower oil

2 tbsp soy sauce

1 tbsp honey

2 tbsp rice vinegar

SALT CHILI
SQUID SALAD

To make the dressing, mix the dressing ingredients together in a
bowl. Cover and refrigerate until required.

   Cut the squid tubes into 2-inch/5-cm pieces, then score
diamond patterns lightly across the flesh with the tip of a
sharp knife. Heat the oil in a wok or large skillet over high heat,
then add the squid pieces and tentacles and stir-fry for 1 minute.
Add the chiles and scallions and stir-fry for another minute.
Season to taste with salt and pepper and add a good squeeze
of lemon juice.

   Mix the watercress and spinach together, then toss with
enough of the dressing to coat lightly. Serve immediately with the
squid, together with lemon wedges to squeeze over the squid.

SERVES 4

12 squid tubes and tentacles
   (about 1 lb 9 oz/700 g total
   weight), cleaned and prepared

2–3 tbsp olive oil

1–2 red chiles, seeded and
   thinly sliced

2 scallions, finely chopped

lemon wedges, for squeezing
   and for serving

3 good handfuls watercress

2 handfuls baby spinach or arugula

salt and pepper

dressing

scant ½ cup olive oil

juice of 1 lime

1 tsp superfine sugar

2 shallots, thinly sliced

1 tomato, peeled, seeded,
   and finely chopped

1 garlic clove, crushed

SPICY WARM CRAB SALAD

SERVES 4

2 sprays sunflower oil

1 fresh serrano chile, seeded and finely chopped

generous 1 cup diagonally halved snow peas

6 scallions, trimmed and finely shredded

2 heaping tbsp frozen corn kernels, defrosted

5½ oz/150 g white crabmeat, drained if canned

2 oz/55 g raw shrimp, peeled and deveined, thawed if frozen

1 large carrot, peeled and grated

¾ cup bean sprouts

8 oz/225 g package fresh baby spinach leaves

1 tbsp finely grated orange rind

2 tbsp orange juice

chopped fresh cilantro, to garnish

Heat a wok and, when hot, spray in the oil and heat for 30 seconds. Add the chile and snow peas then stir-fry over medium heat for 2 minutes.

Add the scallions and corn and continue to stir-fry for another 1 minute.

Add the crabmeat, shrimp, carrot, bean sprouts, and spinach leaves. Stir in the orange rind and juice and stir-fry for 2–3 minutes, or until the spinach has begun to wilt and everything is cooked. Serve divided equally among 4 bowls, sprinkled with the chopped cilantro.

FRUIT

CHILLED BERRY BREAKFAST SALAD

Put all the berries into a shallow bowl. Stir in the orange juice and sugar. Cover and chill in the refrigerator for at least 2 hours or overnight.

Put the yogurt into a small bowl and fold in the orange rind and honey.

Divide the chilled salad among 4 serving bowls. Top each with a spoonful of the yogurt mixture and sprinkle with the sunflower seeds and hazelnuts. Serve immediately.

SERVES 4

2 cups small strawberries, halved

scant 1 cup raspberries

scant 1 cup blackberries

1 cup blueberries

juice and finely grated rind of
    1 orange

1 tbsp superfine sugar

6 tbsp strained plain yogurt

1 tbsp orange blossom honey

1 tbsp sunflower seeds

1 tbsp toasted chopped hazelnuts

GREEN FRUIT
SALAD

To make the syrup, pare the rind from the orange using a vegetable peeler.

Put the orange rind in a pan with the white wine, water, and honey. Bring to a boil, then simmer gently for 10 minutes.

Remove the syrup from the heat. Add the mint sprigs and set aside to cool.

To prepare the fruit, first cut the melon in half and scoop out the seeds. Use a melon baller or a teaspoon to make melon balls.

Core and chop the apples. Peel and slice the kiwis.

Strain the cooled syrup into a serving bowl, removing and reserving the orange rind and discarding the mint sprigs.

Add the apple, grapes, kiwis, and melon to the serving bowl. Stir through gently to mix.

Serve the fruit salad, decorated with sprigs of fresh mint and some of the reserved orange rind.

SERVES 4

1 honeydew melon

2 green apples

2 kiwis

1 cup seedless white grapes

fresh mint sprigs, to decorate

syrup dressing

1 orange

$^2/_3$ cup white wine

$^2/_3$ cup water

4 tbsp honey

fresh mint sprigs

TROPICAL FRUIT SALAD

SERVES 4

1 papaya

1 mango

1 pineapple

4 oranges, peeled and cut into segments

1 cup hulled and quartered strawberries

light or heavy cream, to serve (optional)

syrup dressing

6 tbsp superfine sugar

1¾ cups water

½ tsp ground allspice

grated rind of ½ lemon

To make the syrup, put all the ingredients into a pan. Bring to a boil, stirring continuously, then continue to boil for 1 minute. Remove from the heat and let cool to room temperature. Transfer to a pitcher or bowl, cover with plastic wrap, and chill in the refrigerator for at least 1 hour.

Peel and halve the papaya and remove the seeds. Cut the flesh into small chunks or slices, and put into a large bowl. Cut the mango twice lengthwise, close to the pit. Remove and discard the pit. Peel and cut the flesh into small chunks or slices, and add to the bowl. Cut off the top and bottom of the pineapple and remove the hard skin. Cut the pineapple in half lengthwise, then into quarters and remove the tough core. Cut the remaining flesh into small pieces and add to the bowl. Add the orange segments and strawberries.

Pour over the chilled syrup, cover with plastic wrap, and chill until required. Serve with light or heavy cream, if using.

EXOTIC FRUIT
COCKTAIL

Cut 1 orange in half and squeeze the juice into a bowl, discarding any seeds. Using a sharp knife, cut away all the peel and pith from the second orange. Working over the bowl to catch the juice, carefully cut the orange segments between the membranes to obtain skinless segments of fruit. Discard any seeds.

Cut the passion fruit in half, scoop the flesh into a nylon strainer, and, using a spoon, push the pulp and juice into the bowl of orange segments. Discard the seeds.

Using a sharp knife, cut away all the skin from the pineapple and cut the flesh lengthwise into quarters. Cut away the central hard core. Cut the flesh into chunks and add to the orange-and-passion fruit mixture. Cover and, if you are not serving at once, let the fruit chill.

Cut the pomegranate into quarters and, using your fingers or a teaspoon, remove the red seeds from the membrane. Cover and let chill until ready to serve—do not add too early to the fruit cocktail because the seeds discolor the other fruit.

Just before serving, peel and slice the banana, add to the fruit cocktail with the pomegranate seeds, and mix thoroughly. Serve at once.

SERVES 6

2 oranges

2 large passion fruit

1 pineapple

1 pomegranate

1 banana

PAPAYA SALAD

To make the dressing, whisk the dressing ingredients together in a bowl. Set aside, stirring occasionally to dissolve the sugar.

Shred the lettuce and white cabbage, then toss together and arrange on a large serving plate.

Peel the papayas and slice them in half. Scoop out the seeds, then slice the flesh thinly. Arrange on top of the lettuce and cabbage.

Soak the tomatoes in a bowl of boiling water for 1 minute, then lift out and peel. Remove the seeds and slice the flesh. Arrange on the salad greens.

Scatter the peanuts and scallions over the top. Whisk the dressing and pour over the salad. Garnish with basil leaves and serve at once.

SERVES 4

1 crisp lettuce

¼ small white cabbage

2 papayas

2 tomatoes

2½ tbsp roughly chopped roasted peanuts

4 scallions, trimmed and sliced thinly

fresh basil leaves, to garnish

dressing

4 tbsp olive oil

1 tbsp fish sauce or light soy sauce

2 tbsp lime or lemon juice

1 tbsp dark brown sugar

1 tsp finely chopped fresh red or green chile

MOROCCAN
ORANGE SALAD

SERVES 4

5 large oranges

1 small red onion, thinly sliced

½ tsp ground cumin

½ tsp ground coriander

1 tbsp coarsely chopped fresh
   flat-leaf parsley

1 tbsp coarsely chopped fresh
   cilantro

salt and pepper

Using a serrated knife, cut off the peel and all the white pith
from 4 of the oranges. Cut the flesh into thin slices, removing any
seeds. Put the orange slices into a shallow dish with the onion.

Halve and squeeze the juice from the remaining orange. Mix
the juice with the cumin and coriander and pour it over the
orange slices. Cover and chill in the refrigerator for 1 hour.

Add the parsley and cilantro to the orange slices and mix
gently. Pile onto a serving dish and season lightly with salt and
pepper before serving.

FENNEL & ORANGE SALAD

Arrange the orange slices in the bottom of a shallow dish. Place a layer of fennel on top and then add a layer of onion.

Mix the orange juice with the vinegar and drizzle over the salad. Season with pepper and serve.

SERVES 4

2 oranges, peeled and sliced

1 bulb Florence fennel, thinly sliced

1 red onion, peeled and sliced into thin rings

pepper

dressing

juice of 1 orange

2 tbsp balsamic vinegar

MELON & MANGO SALAD

To make the melon dressing, whisk the dressing ingredients together in a bowl.

Halve the melon, scoop out the seeds with a spoon, and discard. Slice, peel, and dice the flesh. Place in a bowl with the grapes.

Slice the mango on each side of its large flat pit. On each mango half, slash the flesh into a crisscross pattern down to, but not through, the skin. Push the skin from underneath to turn the mango halves inside out. Now remove the flesh and add to the melon mixture.

Arrange the watercress and lettuce leaves on 4 serving plates.

To make the salad greens dressing, whisk the dressing ingredients together in a bowl. Drizzle over the salad greens.

Divide the melon mixture among the 4 plates and spoon the melon dressing over it.

Scoop the seeds out of the passion fruit and sprinkle them over the salads. Serve immediately or chill in the refrigerator until required.

SERVES 4

1 cantaloupe melon

½ cup halved and seeded black grapes

½ cup green grapes

1 large mango

1 bunch watercress, trimmed

iceberg lettuce leaves, shredded

1 passion fruit

melon dressing

⅔ cup plain yogurt

1 tbsp honey

1 tsp grated fresh ginger

salad green

salad greens dressing

2 tbsp olive oil

1 tbsp apple vinegar

salt and pepper

MELON & STRAWBERRY SALAD

SERVES 4

½ iceberg lettuce, shredded

1 small honeydew melon

2 cups strawberries, sliced

2-inch/5-cm piece cucumber, thinly sliced

fresh mint sprigs, to garnish

dressing

scant 1 cup plain yogurt

2-inch/5-cm piece cucumber, peeled

a few fresh mint leaves

½ tsp finely grated lime or lemon rind

pinch of superfine sugar

3–4 ice cubes

Arrange the shredded lettuce on 4 serving plates.

Cut the melon lengthwise into quarters. Scoop out the seeds and cut through the flesh down to the skin at 1-inch/2.5-cm intervals. Cut the melon close to the skin and detach the flesh.

Place the chunks of melon on the beds of lettuce with the strawberry and cucumber slices.

To make the dressing, put all the ingredients into a blender or food processor. Blend together for about 15 seconds, until smooth.

Serve the salad with a little dressing poured over it. Garnish with sprigs of fresh mint.

MINTED PEA & MELON SALAD

Cut the flesh from all the melons into even chunks, removing any seeds. Put the chunks into a bowl with the cucumber.

To make the dressing, whisk the dressing ingredients together in a separate bowl.

Pour the dressing over the melons and cucumber and toss well to coat. Cover and chill for 1 hour.

Add the pea shoots to the chilled melons and cucumber and gently toss together. Transfer to a serving bowl and serve garnished with mint leaves.

FRUIT

286

SERVES 4

1 large wedge watermelon

½ small honeydew melon

½ Charentais or cantaloupe melon

½ cucumber, peeled and diced

1 cup fresh pea shoots

fresh mint leaves, to garnish

dressing

3 tbsp light olive oil

1 tbsp white wine vinegar

½ tsp superfine sugar

1 tbsp chopped fresh mint

salt and pepper

PROSCIUTTO WITH MELON & ASPARAGUS

Trim the asparagus, cutting in half if very long. Cook in lightly salted boiling water over medium heat for 5 minutes, or until tender. Drain and plunge into cold water, then drain again and set aside.

Cut the melon in half and scoop out the seeds. Cut into small wedges and cut away the rind. Separate the prosciutto slices, cut in half, and wrap around the melon wedges.

Arrange the salad greens on a large serving platter and place the melon wedges on top together with the asparagus spears.

Scatter over the raspberries and Parmesan shavings. To make the dressing, place all the ingredients in a screw-top jar and shake vigorously until they are well blended. Pour over the salad and serve.

SERVES 4

8 oz/225 g asparagus spears

1 small or ½ medium Galia or cantaloupe melon

2 oz/55 g prosciutto, thinly sliced

5½ oz/150 g package mixed salad greens, such as herb salad with arugula

generous ½ cup fresh raspberries

1 tbsp freshly shaved Parmesan cheese

dressing

1 tbsp balsamic vinegar

2 tbsp raspberry vinegar

2 tbsp orange juice

CANTALOUPE & CRAB SALAD

SERVES 4

12 oz/350 g fresh crabmeat

5 tbsp mayonnaise

¼ cup plain yogurt

4 tsp extra virgin olive oil

4 tsp lime juice

1 scallion, finely chopped

4 tsp finely chopped fresh flat-leaf parsley

pinch of cayenne pepper

1 cantaloupe melon

2 radicchio heads, separated into leaves

fresh flat-leaf parsley sprigs, to garnish

fresh crusty bread, to serve

Place the crabmeat in a large bowl and pick over it very carefully to remove any remaining shell or cartilage, but try not to break up the meat.

Put the mayonnaise, yogurt, olive oil, lime juice, scallion, chopped fresh parsley, and cayenne pepper into a separate bowl and mix until thoroughly blended. Fold in the crabmeat.

Cut the melon in half and remove and discard the seeds. Slice into wedges, then cut off the rind with a sharp knife.

Arrange the melon slices and radicchio leaves on a plate, then arrange the crabmeat mixture on top. Garnish with a few sprigs of fresh parsley and serve with fresh crusty bread.

FRUIT

291

FIG & WATERMELON SALAD

Cut the watermelon into quarters and scoop out and discard the seeds. Cut the flesh away from the rind, then chop the flesh into 1-inch/2.5-cm cubes. Place the watermelon cubes in a bowl with the grapes. Cut each fig lengthwise into 8 wedges and add to the bowl.

To make the dressing, grate the lime rind and mix it with the orange rind and juice, maple syrup, and honey in a small pan. Bring to a boil over low heat. Pour the mixture over the fruit and stir. Let cool. Stir again, cover, and let chill in the refrigerator for at least 1 hour, stirring occasionally.

Divide the fruit salad equally among 4 bowls and serve.

SERVES 4

1 watermelon, weighing about
  3 lb 5 oz/1.5 kg

¾ cup seeded black grapes

4 figs

syrup dressing

1 lime

grated rind and juice of 1 orange

1 tbsp maple syrup

2 tbsp honey

SPRING CLEAN
SALAD

Place the apples in a bowl and pour over the lemon juice. Mix well to prevent discoloration.

Add the rest of the fruit and vegetables to the bowl and mix gently. Pour in the walnut oil, mix again, and serve.

SERVES 4

2 apples, cored and diced

juice of 1 lemon

large chunk of watermelon, seeded and cubed

1 head Belgian endive, sliced into rounds

4 celery stalks with leaves, coarsely chopped

1 tbsp walnut oil

RASPBERRY & FETA SALAD

SERVES 6

2 cups couscous

2½ cups boiling chicken stock
   or vegetable stock

2 cups fresh raspberries

small bunch of fresh basil

1½ cups crumbled or cubed feta
   cheese

2 zucchini, thinly sliced

4 scallions, trimmed and
   diagonally sliced

⅓ cup pine nuts, toasted

grated rind of 1 lemon

dressing

1 tbsp white wine vinegar

1 tbsp balsamic vinegar

4 tbsp extra virgin olive oil

juice of 1 lemon

salt and pepper

Put the couscous in a large heatproof bowl and pour over the stock. Stir well, then cover and let soak until all the stock has been absorbed.

Pick over the raspberries, discarding any that are overripe. Shred the basil leaves.

Transfer the couscous to a large serving bowl and stir well to break up any lumps. Add the cheese, zucchini, scallions, raspberries, and pine nuts. Stir in the basil and lemon rind and gently toss all the ingredients together.

To make the dressing, place all the ingredients in a screw-top jar and shake vigorously until they are well blended. Pour over the salad and serve.

FRUIT

STRAWBERRY & WATERCRESS SALAD

To make the glaze, put the vinegar and sugar into a small pan. Heat gently, stirring, until the sugar dissolves. Simmer gently for 5–6 minutes, until syrupy. Let cool for 30 minutes.

Put the watercress into a serving dish. Sprinkle with the strawberries. Halve, pit, peel, and slice the avocado and toss gently in the lemon juice. Add to the salad. Sprinkle with the cucumber and walnuts.

Drizzle the glaze over the salad. Season lightly with salt and pepper and serve immediately.

SERVES 4

1 bunch watercress, tough stalks removed

scant 2½ cups sliced strawberries

1 ripe avocado

1 tbsp lemon juice

¼ cucumber, finely diced

1 tbsp chopped walnuts

salt and pepper

balsamic glaze

1 tbsp balsamic vinegar

1 tbsp sugar

FETA, MINT & STRAWBERRY SALAD

To make the dressing, mix the vinegar, sugar, mustard, and salt together in a bowl until smooth. Slowly pour in the oil, whisking constantly until the mixture has emulsified. Cover and refrigerate until required.

Blanch the beans in a large saucepan of salted boiling water for 1–2 minutes, so that they retain plenty of crunch. Drain and quickly toss in a large, cool bowl. Hull and halve the strawberries, then add to the beans. Stir in the pistachios and mint leaves. Toss the salad with enough of the dressing to coat lightly.

Break the feta cheese into chunks and scatter over the salad. Add a good grinding of pepper and serve immediately.

SERVES 4–6

1 lb 2 oz/500 g fine green beans

1 lb 2 oz/500 g strawberries

2–3 tbsp pistachios

1 small bunch fresh mint leaves

1 lb 2 oz/500 g feta cheese (drained weight)

pepper

dressing

2 tbsp raspberry vinegar

2 tsp superfine sugar

1 tbsp Dijon mustard

pinch of salt

½ cup olive oil

WARM PEACH & GOAT CHEESE SALAD

SERVES 4

4 just ripe peaches, halved, pitted and cut into 6 slices

1 tbsp olive oil

2 tsp lemon juice

2 oz/55 g corn salad

2 oz/55 g frisée

4½ oz/125 g mild goat cheese, crumbled

4 slices Serrano ham

1 tbsp toasted hazelnuts, chopped

dressing

4 tbsp olive oil

2 tbsp hazelnut oil

2 tbsp red wine vinegar

½ tsp sugar

salt and pepper

To make the dressing, whisk the dressing ingredients together in a bowl.

Place the peach slices in a separate bowl and add the olive oil and lemon juice. Turn to coat and season lightly with salt and pepper.

Heat a cast-iron griddle pan and add the peach slices. Cook over a medium heat for 2–3 minutes, turning once, until lightly charred and just starting to soften.

Mix the corn salad and frisée together in a bowl and add half the dressing. Toss well to coat and divide between 4 serving plates. Top with the warm peach slices and crumbled goat cheese. Place a ruffled slice of ham on the top of each salad.

Drizzle over the rest of the dressing and scatter over the toasted hazelnuts. Serve immediately.

FRUIT

303

PEAR & ROQUEFORT SALAD

To make the dressing, place the cheese in a bowl and mash with a fork. Gradually blend the yogurt into the cheese to make a smooth consistency. Add the chives and season with pepper to taste.

Tear the lollo rosso, radicchio, and mâche leaves into manageable pieces. Arrange the salad greens on a large serving platter or divide them among individual serving plates.

Cut the pears into quarters and remove the cores. Cut the quarters into slices. Arrange the pear slices over the salad leaves.

Drizzle the dressing over the pears and garnish with a few whole chives.

SERVES 4

few leaves lollo rosso

few leaves radicchio

few leaves mâche

2 ripe pears

whole fresh chives, to garnish

dressing

2 oz/55 g Roquefort cheese

²/₃ cup plain yogurt

2 tbsp chopped fresh chives

pepper

PEAR & BLEU CHEESE SALAD

Bring a large pan of lightly salted water to a boil. Add the pasta and return to a boil. Cook for 8–10 minutes, until just tender, or according to package directions. Drain and set aside.

Place the radicchio and oak leaf lettuce leaves in a large bowl. Halve the pears, remove the cores, and dice the flesh. Toss the diced pear with the lemon juice in a small bowl to prevent discoloration. Top the salad with the bleu cheese, walnuts, pears, pasta, tomatoes, onion slices, corn, and grated carrot. Add the basil and corn salad.

To make the dressing, mix the dressing ingredients together in a separate bowl. Pour the dressing over the salad, toss, and serve.

SERVES 4

9 oz/250 g dried orecchiette

1 head radicchio, torn into pieces

1 oak leaf lettuce, torn into pieces

2 pears

1 tbsp lemon juice

9 oz/250 g bleu cheese, diced

scant ½ cup chopped walnuts

4 tomatoes, quartered

1 red onion, sliced

1 cup canned corn kernels, drained

1 carrot, grated

8 fresh basil leaves

2 oz/55 g corn salad

dressing

4 tbsp olive oil

2 tbsp lemon juice

salt and pepper

BEAN SPROUT, APRICOT & ALMOND SALAD

SERVES 4

1²⁄₃ cups bean sprouts, washed and dried

small bunch seedless black and green grapes, halved

12 unsulfured dried apricots, halved

¼ cup blanched almonds, halved

pepper

dressing

1 tbsp walnut oil

1 tsp sesame oil

2 tsp balsamic vinegar

Place the bean sprouts in the bottom of a large salad bowl and sprinkle the grapes and apricots on top.

To make the dressing, place all the ingredients in a screw-top jar and shake vigorously until they are well blended. Pour over the salad.

Scatter over the almonds and season with pepper.

CHICKEN & GRAPEFRUIT SALAD

Put the chicken into a large pan and pour in enough water to cover. Add the bouquet garni and peppercorns and bring to a gentle simmer. Cover and simmer for 25–30 minutes, until just cooked through. Let the chicken cool in the liquid.

Using a serrated knife, cut away the peel and pith from the grapefruits. Holding the fruit over a bowl to catch any juice, segment the flesh. Reserve 2 tbsp of the juice.

Toss the salad greens in a bowl with the grapefruit segments.

To make the dressing, put all the ingredients into a bowl with the reserved grapefruit juice. Whisk together until thoroughly blended.

Drain the poached chicken and pat dry with paper towels. Tear into bite-size strips or thinly slice. Arrange on top of the salad. Drizzle with the dressing and season with a little more pepper to serve. Serve garnished with sprigs of fresh chervil.

SERVES 4

2 skinless, boneless chicken breasts, about 6 oz/175 g each

1 bouquet garni

few black peppercorns

2 pink grapefruits

3 Boston lettuce, separated into leaves

1 head endive, separated into leaves

fresh chervil sprigs, to garnish

dressing

1 tbsp light olive oil

3 tbsp strained plain yogurt

1 tsp whole-grain mustard

pinch of sugar

1 tbsp chopped fresh chervil

salt and pepper

CHICKEN & CRANBERRY SALAD

Carve the chicken carefully, slicing the white meat. Divide the legs into thighs and drumsticks and trim the wings. Cover with plastic wrap and refrigerate.

Put the cranberries in a bowl. Stir in the apple juice, then cover with plastic wrap and let soak for 30 minutes.

Meanwhile, blanch the sugar snap peas, then refresh under cold running water and drain.

Peel, pit, and slice the avocados and toss in the lemon juice to prevent discoloration.

Separate the lettuce hearts and arrange on a large serving platter with the avocados, sugar snap peas, watercress, arugula, and the chicken.

To make the dressing, place all the ingredients in a screw-top jar and shake vigorously until they are well blended.

Drain the cranberries and mix them with the dressing, then pour over the salad. Serve immediately.

SERVES 4

1 cooked smoked chicken, weighing 3 lb/1.3 kg

scant 1 cup dried cranberries

2 tbsp apple juice or water

3 cups sugar snap peas

2 ripe avocados

juice of ½ lemon

4 lettuce hearts

1 bunch watercress, trimmed

2¾ cups arugula

dressing

2 tbsp olive oil

1 tbsp walnut oil

2 tbsp lemon juice

1 tbsp chopped fresh mixed herbs, such as parsley and lemon thyme

salt and pepper

SHRIMP WITH PINEAPPLE & PAPAYA SALSA

SERVES 8

4 tbsp sunflower oil

1 fresh red chile, seeded and chopped

1 garlic clove, crushed

48 shrimp

chopped fresh flat-leaf parsley, to garnish

pineapple & papaya salsa

1 large papaya, halved, seeded, peeled, and cut into ¼-inch/5 mm dice

1 small pineapple, halved, cored, peeled, and cut into ¼ inch/5 mm dice

2 scallions, very finely chopped

1 fresh red chile, or to taste, seeded and finely chopped

1 garlic clove, very finely chopped

2½ tsp lemon juice

½ tsp ground cumin

¼ tsp salt

pepper

To make the salsa, put all the ingredients in a large bowl. Adjust the lemon juice, cumin, salt and pepper to taste, if necessary. Cover and chill until required, ideally at least 2 hours.

Heat a wok over high heat. Add the oil and swirl around, then add the chile and garlic and stir-fry for 20 seconds. Add the shrimp and stir-fry for 2–3 minutes, until the shrimp are cooked through, become pink and curl.

Tip the shrimp, chile, garlic and any oil left in the wok into a heatproof bowl and let the shrimp cool and marinate in the chile oil. When the shrimp are completely cool, cover the bowl and chill for at least 2 hours.

When ready to serve, give the salsa a stir and adjust the seasoning, if necessary. Arrange a mound of salsa on each of 8 plates. Remove the shrimp from the marinade and divide among plates. Sprinkle with parsley and serve.

FRUIT

315

INDEX

alfalfa sprouts: tuna with bean sprouts
  salad 260
almonds
  bean sprout, apricot & almond salad 309
  chicken & spinach salad 253
  Chinese chicken salad 85
  coronation chicken salad 70
anchovies
  anchovy & olive salad 143
  caesar salad 140
  chicken and pancetta caesar salad 80
  salad niçoise 120
apples
  green fruit salad 270
  nutty beet salad 223
  red cabbage & beet slaw 214
  spring clean salad 294
  steak waldorf salad 28
apricots
  bean sprout, apricot & almond salad 309
  turkey couscous salad 104
artichokes
  artichoke & prosciutto salad 49
  artichoke & spicy sausage salad 61
arugula
  asparagus & tomato salad 181
  chicken & cheese salad 73
  chicken & cranberry salad 312
  coronation chicken salad 70
  ham & salami salad with figs 50
  herbed mixed bean salad 196
  honey & chicken pasta salad 98
  new potato & radish salad 184
  roast pork & pumpkin salad 38
  salad with garlic dressing 220
  salt chili squid salad 262
  smoked salmon & arugula salad 132
  soybean & mushroom salad 242
  tuna, lentil & potato salad 125
  warm mackerel & potato salad 144
asparagus
  asparagus & tomato salad 181
  prosciutto with melon & asparagus 288
  tuna & herbed pasta salad 128
avocados
  BLT salad 32
  chicken avocado salad 76
  chicken & cranberry salad 312
  chicken fajita salad 97
  lobster & summer herb salad 161
  smoked chicken salad 74
  smoked salmon & arugula salad 132
  strawberry & watercress salad 298
  tomato & mozzarella salad 176
  tuna & avocado salad 259

bacon
  BLT salad 32
  crispy spinach & bacon salad 34
  walnut, pear & crispy bacon salad 37
  warm bacon & egg salad 31
  see also pancetta
bananas: exotic fruit cocktail 274
bang bang chicken salad 86
basil
  basil, chive & lemon vinegar 17
  chickpea & tomato salad 236
  duck & radish salad 112
  fruity cottage cheese salad 244
  ham & salami salad with figs 50
  marinated bell pepper salad 200
  pasta salad with bell peppers 199
  raspberry & feta salad 297
  roast duck salad 109
  roasted vegetable salad 172
  seared swordfish with salsa 146
  sun-dried tomato salad 178

tuna & herbed pasta salad 128
Tuscan bread salad 175
bbq chicken salad 94
bean sprouts
  bang bang chicken salad 86
  bean sprout, apricot & almond salad 309
  caramelized tuna salad 122
  Indonesian warm salad 247
  roast duck salad 109
  smoked chicken salad 74
  spicy warm crab salad 265
  Thai crab patty salad 158
  Thai-style chicken salad 254
  tuna with bean sprouts salad 260
  vegetable & rice noodle salad 248
beans 10
  see also cannellini beans; cranberry beans;
    kidney beans; lima beans
beef
  beef satay salad 25
  roast beef salad 22
  steak waldorf salad 28
  Sichuan numbing beef salad 26
  warm beef salad niçoise 20
beets
  bell pepper & radicchio salad 232
  Cajun chicken salad 92
  nutty beet salad 223
  red cabbage & beet slaw 214
  three bean salad 241
bell peppers
  bbq chicken salad 94
  bell pepper & radicchio salad 232
  chicken fajita salad 97
  fruity cottage cheese salad 244
  gingered chicken salad 88
  layered chicken salad 68
  marinated bell pepper salad 200
  pasta salad with bell peppers 199
  pastrami & bell pepper antipasti salad 46
  roast chicken with pesto cream salad 79
  roast duck salad 109
  roasted vegetable salad 172
  salad with garlic dressing 220
  salami pasta salad 52
  spicy sausage pasta salad 56
  succatash salad 230
  sweet potato salad 188
  sweet & sour fish salad 149
  teriyaki salmon salad 134
  tuna & avocado salad 259
  tuna & herbed pasta salad 128
  turkey salad pockets 256
  vegetable & rice noodle salad 248
  warm beef salad niçoise 20
  warm oriental-style salad 250
  watercress, zucchini & mint salad 235
  wild rice salad 202
blackberries: chilled berry breakfast
  salad 268
blanching vegetables 12
BLT salad 32
blueberries: chilled berry breakfast
  salad 268
bok choy: warm oriental-style salad 250
Boston lettuce
  bbq chicken salad 94
  caesar salad 140
  chicken & grapefruit salad 310
  layered crayfish salad 156
  roast duck salad 109
  tuna, lentil & potato salad 125
bread
  caesar salad 140
  chicken & pancetta caesar salad 80
  crispy spinach & bacon salad 34
  goat cheese crouton & spinach salad 208

shrimp & white bean salad 152
Tuscan bread salad 175
warm bacon & egg salad 31
broccoli
  cauliflower, broccoli & cashew nut
    salad 182
  vegetable & rice noodle salad 248
  warm oriental-style salad 250
buckwheat noodle salad 212
bulgur wheat salad 224

cabbage
  buckwheat noodle salad 212
  papaya salad 276
  red cabbage & beet slaw 214
caesar salad 140
Cajun chicken salad 92
cannellini beans
  herbed mixed bean salad 196
  shrimp & white bean salad 152
  three bean salad 241
  tuna & two-bean salad 126
cantaloupe & crab salad 291
capers
  seared swordfish with salsa 146
  sun-dried tomato salad 178
  Tuscan bread salad 175
carrots
  bang bang chicken salad 86
  bbq chicken salad 94
  braised chicken salad 100
  buckwheat noodle salad 212
  duck & noodle salad with peanut sauce 116
  hoisin pork with ribbon salad 40
  Indonesian warm salad 247
  layered crayfish salad 156
  noodle baskets with chicken salad 91
  pear & bleu cheese salad 306
  spiced orange & carrot salad 205
  spicy warm crab salad 265
  sweet potato & bean salad 190
  teriyaki salmon salad 134
  turkey salad pockets 256
  warm oriental-style salad 250
cashew nuts
  cauliflower, broccoli & cashew nut
    salad 182
  coronation chicken salad 70
  three bean salad 241
  warm oriental-style salad 250
cauliflower, broccoli & cashew nut
  salad 182
celery
  braised chicken salad 100
  chicken avocado salad 76
  chicken & cheese salad 73
  chicken & spinach salad 253
  duck & noodle salad with peanut sauce 116
  duck & radish salad 112
  duck salad with sweet chili dressing 115
  roast chicken with pesto cream salad 79
  salad with garlic dressing 220
  shrimp & white bean salad 152
  spring clean salad 294
  steak waldorf salad 28
  sweet potato & bean salad 190
  watercress, zucchini & mint salad 235
cheese
  BLT salad 32
  chicken & cheese salad 73
  chili spiced paneer salad 211
  fruity cottage cheese salad 244
  herbed mixed bean salad 196
  pear & bleu cheese salad 306
  pear & Roquefort salad 304
  see also feta cheese; goat cheese;
    mozzarella cheese; Parmesan cheese

chicken
  bang bang chicken salad 86
  bbq chicken salad 94
  braised chicken salad 100
  Cajun chicken salad 92
  chicken avocado salad 76
  chicken & cheese salad 73
  chicken & cranberry salad 312
  chicken fajita salad 97
  chicken & grapefruit salad 310
  chicken & pancetta caesar salad 80
  chicken, raisin & pine nut salad 103
  chicken & spinach salad 253
  Chinese chicken salad 85
  coronation chicken salad 70
  gingered chicken salad 88
  honey & chicken pasta salad 98
  layered chicken salad 68
  noodle baskets with chicken salad 91
  roast chicken with pesto cream salad 79
  smoked chicken salad 74
  Thai-style chicken salad 254
chicken livers: warm chicken liver salad 82
chickpea & tomato salad 236
chiles
  beef satay salad 25
  buckwheat noodle salad 212
  caramelized tuna salad 122
  chickpea & tomato salad 236
  chili spiced paneer salad 211
  fruity cottage cheese salad 244
  garlic, chile & oregano oil 14
  papaya salad 276
  pork & cucumber salad 43
  salt chili squid salad 262
  seafood & spinach salad 164
  shrimp with pineapple & papaya salsa 315
  spiced fish skewers & tomato salad 150
  spicy warm crab salad 265
  sweet & sour fish salad 149
  Thai-style chicken salad 254
  tuna & avocado salad 259
  warm oriental-style salad 250
  see also sweet chili sauce
Chinese cabbage
  bang bang chicken salad 86
  beef satay salad 25
  Chinese chicken salad 85
  duck & radish salad 112
Chinese chicken salad 85
chives
  broiled lamb with yogurt dressing 62
  chicken avocado salad 76
  fruity cottage cheese salad 244
  layered chicken salad 68
  Neapolitan seafood salad 167
  pear & Roquefort salad 304
  soybean & mushroom salad 242
  turkey & rice salad 106
cilantro
  caramelized tuna salad 122
  cauliflower, broccoli & cashew nut
    salad 182
  chicken fajita salad 97
  chili spiced paneer salad 211
  coconut shrimp salad 155
  green bean salad with feta 193
  lamb kofte & herb salad 64
  Moroccan orange salad 279
  noodle baskets with chicken salad 91
  parsley & cilantro oil 15
  pork & cucumber salad 43
  seafood & spinach salad 164
  spiced fish skewers & tomato salad 150
  spiced orange & carrot salad 205
  tabbouleh 226
  Thai crab patty salad 158

Thai-style chicken salad 254
three bean salad 241
turkey couscous salad 104
turkey & rice salad 106
warm red lentil salad 206
cockles: Neapolitan seafood salad 167
coconut
  beef satay salad 25
  cauliflower, broccoli & cashew nut
    salad 182
  coconut shrimp salad 155
  duck & noodle salad with peanut
    sauce 116
  Indonesian warm salad 247
cod
  spiced fish skewers & tomato salad 150
  sweet & sour fish salad 149
corn
  bbq chicken salad 94
  gingered chicken salad 88
  layered crayfish salad 156
  spicy warm crab salad 265
  succatash salad 230
  Thai-style chicken salad 254
  vegetable & rice noodle salad 248
  warm oriental-style salad 250
cornichons: new potato & radish salad 184
corn salad
  asparagus & tomato salad 181
  warm peach & goat cheese salad 303
coronation chicken salad 70
couscous
  raspberry & feta salad 297
  turkey couscous salad 104
crabmeat
  cantaloupe & crab salad 291
  spicy warm crab salad 265
  Thai crab patty salad 158
cranberries
  chicken & cranberry salad 312
  three bean salad 241
cranberry beans: sweet potato & bean
   salad 190
crayfish: layered crayfish salad 156
cress: Thai crab patty salad 158
cress: tuna with bean sprouts salad 260
cucumber
  bang bang chicken salad 86
  beef satay salad 25
  BLT salad 32
  bulgur wheat salad 224
  caramelized tuna salad 122
  chicken & cheese salad 73
  chicken & spinach salad 253
  coconut shrimp salad 155
  duck & noodle salad with peanut sauce 116
  gingered chicken salad 88
  Greek feta salad 218
  hoisin pork with ribbon salad 40
  Indonesian warm salad 247
  lamb kofte & herb salad 64
  layered crayfish salad 156
  melon & strawberry salad 285
  minted pea & melon salad 286
  noodle baskets with chicken salad 91
  pork & cucumber salad 43
  roast duck salad 109
  salad with garlic dressing 220
  strawberry & watercress salad 298
  tabbouleh 226
  Thai crab patty salad 158
  traditional Greek salad 170
  Tuscan bread salad 175
  warm salmon & mango salad 137
  wild rice salad 202
curry paste
  cauliflower, broccoli & cashew nut

salad 182
coronation chicken salad 70
Thai crab patty salad 158

dill
  new potato & radish salad 184
  nutty beet salad 223
  warm mackerel & potato salad 144
duck
  duck & noodle salad with peanut sauce 116
  duck & radish salad 112
  duck salad with sweet chili dressing 115
  roast duck salad 109
  warm duck, shallot & orange salad 110

eggplants
  roasted vegetable salad 172
  sweet potato salad 188
eggs
  caesar salad 140
  Indonesian warm salad 247
  salad niçoise 120
  warm bacon & egg salad 31
  warm beef salad niçoise 20
endive
  braised chicken salad 100
  chicken & grapefruit salad 310
  smoked trout, endive & pear salad 138
  spring clean salad 294

fava beans: herbed mixed bean salad 196
fennel & orange salad 280
feta cheese
  feta, mint & strawberry salad 300
  Greek feta salad 218
  green bean salad with feta 193
  quinoa salad with sun-dried tomatoes 229
  raspberry & feta salad 297
  roast pork & pumpkin salad 38
  three bean salad 241
  traditional Greek salad 170
figs
  fig & watermelon salad 292
  ham & salami salad with figs 50
flageolets: three bean salad 241

ginger
  buckwheat noodle salad 212
  caramelized tuna salad 122
  chicken & spinach salad 253
  gingered chicken salad 88
  melon & mango salad 282
  noodle baskets with chicken salad 91
  roast duck salad 109
  seafood & spinach salad 164
  teriyaki salmon salad 134
  tuna with bean sprouts salad 260
  vegetable & rice noodle salad 248
  warm oriental-style salad 250
  warm red lentil salad 206
goat cheese
  goat cheese crouton & spinach salad 208
  warm peach & goat cheese salad 303
  warm red lentil salad 206
grapefruits: chicken & grapefruit salad 310
grapes
  bean sprout, apricot & almond salad 309
  chicken & cheese salad 73
  fig & watermelon salad 292
  fruity cottage cheese salad 244
  green fruit salad 270
  melon & mango salad 282
  smoked trout, endive & pear salad 138
Greek feta salad 218
Greek salad 170
green beans
  feta, mint & strawberry salad 300

green bean salad with feta 193
green bean & walnut salad 194
herbed mixed bean salad 196
Indonesian warm salad 247
minted pea & green bean rice salad 238
roast beef salad 22
roast pork & pumpkin salad 38
salad niçoise 120
succatash salad 230
tuna & two-bean salad 126
warm beef salad niçoise 20
watercress, zucchini & mint salad 235

haddock: sweet & sour fish salad 149
ham
ham & salami salad with figs 50
warm peach & goat cheese salad 303
harissa paste
onion & herb salad with spicy sausage 55
turkey couscous salad 104
hazelnuts
chilled berry breakfast salad 268
roast beef salad 22
warm peach & goat cheese salad 303
herbs 8, 11
see also basil; dill; mint; parsley; tarragon;
thyme
hoisin pork with ribbon salad 40
honey
bbq chicken salad 94
chicken & spinach salad 253
chilled berry breakfast salad 268
fig & watermelon salad 292
fruity cottage cheese salad 244
green fruit salad 270
honey & chicken pasta salad 98
hot sausage & potato salad 58
melon & mango salad 282
sweet & sour fish salad 149
tuna & herbed pasta salad 128
tuna with bean sprouts salad 260
hot sausage & potato salad 58
hummus: turkey salad pockets 256

iceberg lettuce
BLT salad 32
duck salad with sweet chili dressing 115
melon & mango salad 282
melon & strawberry salad 285
pastrami & bell pepper antipasti salad 46
pork & cucumber salad 43
roast chicken with pesto cream salad 79
traditional Greek salad 170
Indonesian warm salad 247

kidney beans: three bean salad 241
kiwis: green fruit salad 270

lamb
broiled lamb with yogurt dressing 62
lamb kofte & herb salad 64
lentils
tuna, lentil & potato salad 125
warm new potato & lentil salad 187
warm red lentil salad 206
lettuce
anchovy & olive salad 143
chicken & cranberry salad 312
papaya salad 276
pear & bleu cheese salad 306
salad niçoise 120
tomato, salmon & shrimp salad 131
traditional Greek salad 170
tuna & two-bean salad 126
see also Boston lettuce; Iceberg lettuce;
lamb's lettuce; romaine lettuce
lima beans: onion & herb salad with spicy
sausage 55

limes
cantaloupe & crab salad 291
chicken fajita salad 97
duck & radish salad 112
fig & watermelon salad 292
fruity cottage cheese salad 244
noodle baskets with chicken salad 91
pork & cucumber salad 43
roast duck salad 109
smoked salmon & arugula salad 132
spiced fish skewers & tomato salad 150
Thai-style chicken salad 254
tuna & herbed pasta salad 128
vegetable & rice noodle salad 248
lobster & summer herb salad 161

mackerel: warm mackerel & potato salad 144
mangoes
Cajun chicken salad 92
coronation chicken salad 70
melon & mango salad 282
tropical fruit salad 273
warm salmon & mango salad 137
melons
artichoke & spicy sausage salad 61
cantaloupe & crab salad 291
fruity cottage cheese salad 244
green fruit salad 270
melon & mango salad 282
melon & strawberry salad 285
minted pea & melon salad 286
prosciutto with melon & asparagus 288
see also watermelon
mint
broiled lamb with yogurt dressing 62
bulgur wheat salad 224
caramelized tuna salad 122
feta, mint & strawberry salad 300
lamb kofte & herb salad 64
melon & strawberry salad 285
minted pea & green bean rice salad 238
minted pea & melon salad 286
noodle baskets with chicken salad 91
pork & cucumber salad 43
roast duck salad 109
tabbouleh 226
tuna & two-bean salad 126
warm red lentil salad 206
watercress, zucchini & mint salad 235
mizuna
asparagus & tomato salad 181
honey & chicken pasta salad 98
monkfish: spiced fish skewers & tomato
salad 150
Moroccan orange salad 279
mozzarella cheese
marinated bell pepper salad 200
salami pasta salad 52
sun-dried tomato salad 178
sweet potato salad 188
tomato & mozzarella salad 176
mushrooms
soybean & mushroom salad 242
spinach & pancetta salad 44
turkey & rice salad 106
mussels
Neapolitan seafood salad 167
seafood salad 162
seafood & spinach salad 164

Neapolitan seafood salad 167
new potato & radish salad 184
noodles
buckwheat noodle salad 212
Chinese chicken salad 85
duck & noodle salad with peanut sauce 116
gingered chicken salad 88

noodle baskets with chicken salad 91
Sichuan numbing beef salad 26
teriyaki salmon salad 134
vegetable & rice noodle salad 248
nuts 10
see also almonds; cashew nuts; hazelnuts;
peanuts; pecan nuts; pistachio nuts;
walnuts

oils 9, 13-15
garlic, chile & oregano oil 14
parsley & cilantro oil 15
olives
anchovy & olive salad 143
artichoke & prosciutto salad 49
asparagus & tomato salad 181
Greek feta salad 218
marinated bell pepper salad 200
pastrami & bell pepper antipasti salad 46
quinoa salad with sun-dried tomatoes 229
roast beef salad 22
salad niçoise 120
salami pasta salad 52
seared swordfish with salsa 146
tomato & mozzarella salad 176
traditional Greek salad 170
warm beef salad niçoise 20
onion & herb salad with spicy sausage 55
oranges
chicken avocado salad 76
chilled berry breakfast salad 268
exotic fruit cocktail 274
fennel & orange salad 280
fig & watermelon salad 292
green fruit salad 270
Moroccan orange salad 279
spiced orange & carrot salad 205
spicy warm crab salad 265
tropical fruit salad 273
warm duck, shallot & orange salad 110
warm salmon & mango salad 137
wild rice salad 202

pancetta
chicken & pancetta caesar salad 80
spinach & pancetta salad 44
paneer: chili spiced paneer salad 211
papayas
papaya salad 276
shrimp with pineapple & papaya salsa 315
tropical fruit salad 273
Parmesan cheese
caesar salad 140
chicken & pancetta caesar salad 80
green bean & walnut salad 194
prosciutto with melon & asparagus 288
roasted vegetable salad 172
parsley
anchovy & olive salad 143
broiled lamb with yogurt dressing 62
bulgur wheat salad 224
cantaloupe & crab salad 291
chicken & cheese salad 73
chicken, raisin & pine nut salad 103
chicken & spinach salad 253
fruity cottage cheese salad 244
herbed mixed bean salad 196
Moroccan orange salad 279
Neapolitan seafood salad 167
noodle baskets with chicken salad 91
parsley & cilantro oil 15
roast pork & pumpkin salad 38
seafood salad 162
shrimp & white bean salad 152
smoked salmon & arugula salad 132
soybean & mushroom salad 242
sun-dried tomato salad 178

tabbouleh 226
tuna & avocado salad 259
tuna & two-bean salad 126
wild rice salad 202
passion fruit
exotic fruit cocktail 274
melon & mango salad 282
pasta 10
honey & chicken pasta salad 98
Neapolitan seafood salad 167
pasta salad with bell peppers 199
pear & bleu cheese salad 306
roast beef salad 22
salami pasta salad 52
spicy sausage pasta salad 56
tuna & herbed pasta salad 128
pastrami & bell pepper antipasti salad 46
peaches: warm peach & goat cheese
salad 303
peanuts
bang bang chicken salad 86
beef satay salad 25
caramelized tuna salad 122
duck & noodle salad with peanut
sauce 116
Indonesian warm salad 247
papaya salad 276
pork & cucumber salad 43
pears
pear & bleu cheese salad 306
pear & Roquefort salad 304
smoked trout, endive & pear salad 138
walnut, pear & crispy bacon salad 37
peas
herbed mixed bean salad 196
minted pea & green bean rice salad 238
minted pea & melon salad 286
pecan nuts: nutty beet salad 223
pesto
pasta salad with bell peppers 199
roast chicken with pesto cream salad 79
salami pasta salad 52
pine nuts
asparagus & tomato salad 181
bulgur wheat salad 224
chicken, raisin & pine nut salad 103
raspberry & feta salad 297
roast pork & pumpkin salad 38
turkey couscous salad 104
pineapple
exotic fruit cocktail 274
shrimp with pineapple & papaya
salsa 315
sweet & sour fish salad 149
tropical fruit salad 273
pistachio nuts
feta, mint & strawberry salad 300
turkey & rice salad 106
pomegranates: exotic fruit cocktail 274
pork
hoisin pork with ribbon salad 40
pork & cucumber salad 43
roast pork & pumpkin salad 38
potatoes
hot sausage & potato salad 58
Indonesian warm salad 247
layered chicken salad 68
new potato & radish salad 184
Thai-style chicken salad 254
tuna & avocado salad 259
tuna, lentil & potato salad 125
warm beef salad niçoise 20
warm mackerel & potato salad 144
warm new potato & lentil salad 187
prosciutto
artichoke & prosciutto salad 49
prosciutto with melon & asparagus 288

pumpkin: roast pork & pumpkin salad 38
pumpkin seeds: red cabbage & beet
slaw 214

quinoa
quinoa salad with sun-dried
tomatoes 229
tabbouleh 226

radicchio
bell pepper & radicchio salad 232
cantaloupe & crab salad 291
pear & bleu cheese salad 306
pear & Roquefort salad 304
roast beef salad 22
radishes
bell pepper & radicchio salad 232
Cajun chicken salad 92
duck & radish salad 112
green bean salad with feta 193
hoisin pork with ribbon salad 40
new potato & radish salad 184
salad with garlic dressing 220
Sichuan numbing beef salad 26
three bean salad 241
raisins
chicken, raisin & pine nut salad 103
spiced orange & carrot salad 205
sweet potato & bean salad 190
raspberries
chilled berry breakfast salad 268
prosciutto with melon & asparagus 288
raspberry & feta salad 297
red cabbage & beet slaw 214
red swiss chard: warm duck, shallot &
orange salad 110
red onions
Cajun chicken salad 92
cauliflower, broccoli & cashew nut
salad 182
chickpea & tomato salad 236
fennel & orange salad 280
fruity cottage cheese salad 244
Greek feta salad 218
green bean salad with feta 193
herbed mixed bean salad 196
marinated bell pepper salad 200
Moroccan orange salad 279
new potato & radish salad 184
pear & bleu cheese salad 306
roast beef salad 22
roast pork & pumpkin salad 38
salami pasta salad 52
seafood salad 162
shrimp & white bean salad 152
Sichuan numbing beef salad 26
three bean salad 241
tuna & herbed pasta salad 128
Tuscan bread salad 175
warm oriental-style salad 250
warm red lentil salad 206
wild rice salad 202
rice 10
coconut shrimp salad 155
minted pea & green bean rice salad 238
turkey & rice salad 106
wild rice salad 202
roast beef salad 22
roast chicken with pesto cream salad 79
roast duck salad 109
roast pork & pumpkin salad 38
roasted vegetable salad 172
romaine lettuce
caesar salad 140
chicken & pancetta caesar salad 80
chickpea & tomato salad 236
Indonesian warm salad 247

traditional Greek salad 170
warm bacon & egg salad 31

salad greens 8, 11
Cajun chicken salad 92
chicken avocado salad 76
chicken fajita salad 97
chili spiced paneer salad 211
fruity cottage cheese salad 244
lamb kofte & herb salad 64
lobster & summer herb salad 161
Neapolitan seafood salad 167
nutty beet salad 223
prosciutto with melon & asparagus 288
spicy sausage pasta salad 56
steak waldorf salad 28
sun-dried tomato salad 178
sweet potato & bean salad 190
sweet potato salad 188
three bean salad 241
warm beef salad niçoise 20
warm chicken liver salad 82
warm salmon & mango salad 137
see also arugula; lettuce; mizuna;
radicchio; watercress
salad niçoise 120
salami
ham & salami salad with figs 50
salami pasta salad 52
spicy sausage pasta salad 56
salmon
teriyaki salmon salad 134
warm salmon & mango salad 137
see also smoked salmon
salt chili squid salad 262
satsumas: chicken avocado salad 76
sausages
hot sausage & potato salad 58
see also spicy sausage
scallions
beef satay salad 25
bell pepper & radicchio salad 232
buckwheat noodle salad 212
chicken & cheese salad 73
chicken & spinach salad 253
chili spiced paneer salad 211
Chinese chicken salad 85
coconut shrimp salad 155
duck salad with sweet chili dressing 115
gingered chicken salad 88
hoisin pork with ribbon salad 40
minted pea & green bean rice salad 238
papaya salad 276
pork & cucumber salad 43
quinoa salad with sun-dried tomatoes 229
raspberry & feta salad 297
salad with garlic dressing 220
salt chili squid salad 262
seafood & spinach salad 164
shrimp with pineapple & papaya salsa 315
smoked salmon & arugula salad 132
spiced orange & carrot salad 205
spicy warm crab salad 265
succatash salad 230
sweet potato & bean salad 190
sweet & sour fish salad 149
tabbouleh 226
teriyaki salmon salad 134
Thai-style chicken salad 254
tuna & two-bean salad 126
warm mackerel & potato salad 144
warm new potato & lentil salad 187
warm salmon & mango salad 137
scallops
seafood & spinach salad 164
seafood salad 162
seafood salad 162

seafood & spinach salad 164
seeds, edible 10
  see also pumpkin seeds; sesame seeds;
    sunflower seeds
sesame seeds
  bang bang chicken salad 86
  broiled lamb with yogurt dressing 62
  buckwheat noodle salad 212
  Cajun chicken salad 92
  Chinese chicken salad 85
  duck & radish salad 112
  hoisin pork with ribbon salad 40
  teriyaki salmon salad 134
  tuna & avocado salad 259
shrimp
  coconut shrimp salad 155
  seafood & spinach salad 164
  shrimp with pineapple & papaya
    salsa 315
  shrimp & white bean salad 152
  spicy warm crab salad 265
  Thai crab patty salad 158
  tomato, salmon & shrimp salad 131
smoked chicken salad 74
smoked salmon
  smoked salmon & arugula salad 132
  tomato, salmon & shrimp salad 131
smoked trout, endive & pear salad 138
snow peas
  gingered chicken salad 88
  minted pea & green bean rice salad 238
  spicy warm crab salad 265
  turkey & rice salad 106
  vegetable & rice noodle salad 248
sour cream
  bbq chicken salad 94
  chicken & pancetta caesar salad 80
  new potato & radish salad 184
  noodle baskets with chicken salad 91
  roast chicken with pesto cream salad 79
soybean & mushroom salad 242
spicy sausage
  artichoke & spicy sausage salad 61
  onion & herb salad with spicy sausage 55
  spicy sausage pasta salad 56
spinach
  braised chicken salad 100
  chicken & spinach salad 253
  coronation chicken salad 70
  crispy spinach & bacon salad 34
  goat cheese crouton & spinach salad 208
  salt chili squid salad 262
  seafood & spinach salad 164
  soybean & mushroom salad 242
  spicy warm crab salad 265
  spinach & pancetta salad 44
  turkey salad pockets 256
  warm duck, shallot & orange salad 110
  warm red lentil salad 206
spring clean salad 294
squid
  Neapolitan seafood salad 167
  salt chili squid salad 262
  seafood salad 162
strawberries
  chilled berry breakfast salad 268
  feta, mint & strawberry salad 300
  melon & strawberry salad 285
  strawberry & watercress salad 298
  tropical fruit salad 273
succatash salad 230
sugar snap peas
  chicken & cranberry salad 312
  duck salad with sweet chili dressing 115
sun-dried tomato salad 178
sunflower seeds
  chicken avocado salad 76
  chilled berry breakfast salad 268

red cabbage & beet slaw 214
turkey salad pockets 256
sweet & sour fish salad 149
sweet chili sauce
  bang bang chicken salad 86
  duck salad with sweet chili dressing 115
  roast duck salad 109
  Thai crab patty salad 158
  vegetable & rice noodle salad 248
sweet potatoes
  sweet potato & bean salad 190
  sweet potato salad 188
swordfish: seared swordfish with salsa 146
Sichuan numbing beef salad 26

tabbouleh 226
tarragon
  artichoke & spicy sausage salad 61
  smoked chicken salad 74
  warm chicken liver salad 82
teriyaki salmon salad 134
Thai crab patty salad 158
Thai-style chicken salad 254
three bean salad 241
thyme: honey & chicken pasta salad 98
tofu: buckwheat noodle salad 212
tomatoes
  anchovy & olive salad 143
  artichoke & prosciutto salad 49
  asparagus & tomato salad 181
  BLT salad 32
  bulgur wheat salad 224
  chicken fajita salad 97
  chickpea & tomato salad 236
  chili spiced paneer salad 211
  goat cheese crouton & spinach salad 208
  Greek feta salad 218
  green bean salad with feta 193
  honey & chicken pasta salad 98
  layered chicken salad 68
  lobster & summer herb salad 161
  onion & herb salad with spicy sausage 55
  papaya salad 276
  pastrami & bell pepper antipasti salad 46
  pear & bleu cheese salad 306
  peeling 12
  quinoa salad with sun-dried tomatoes 229
  salad with garlic dressing 220
  salad niçoise 120
  salami pasta salad 52
  seared swordfish with salsa 146
  shrimp & white bean salad 152
  smoked chicken salad 74
  spiced fish skewers & tomato salad 150
  sun-dried tomato salad 178
  sweet potato & bean salad 190
  tabbouleh 226
  three bean salad 241
  tomato & mozzarella salad 176
  tomato, salmon & shrimp salad 131
  traditional Greek salad 170
  tuna & avocado salad 259
  tuna & herbed pasta salad 128
  tuna, lentil & potato salad 125
  tuna & two-bean salad 126
  Tuscan bread salad 175
  warm bacon & egg salad 31
  warm beef salad niçoise 20
  warm salmon & mango salad 137
  wild rice salad 202
top tips for perfect salads 11–12
tropical fruit salad 273
trout
  smoked trout, endive & pear salad 138
  sweet & sour fish salad 149
tuna
  caramelized tuna salad 122
  salad niçoise 120

tuna & avocado salad 259
tuna & herbed pasta salad 128
tuna, lentil & potato salad 125
tuna with bean sprouts salad 260
tuna & two-bean salad 126
turkey
  turkey couscous salad 104
  turkey & rice salad 106
  turkey salad pockets 256
Tuscan bread salad 175

vinegars 9, 16–17
  basil, chive & lemon vinegar 17
  rosemary & garlic balsamic vinegar 17

walnuts
  Cajun chicken salad 92
  chicken & cheese salad 73
  green bean & walnut salad 194
  pear & bleu cheese salad 306
  steak waldorf salad 28
  strawberry & watercress salad 298
  walnut, pear & crispy bacon salad 37
  warm bacon & egg salad 31
  warm beef salad niçoise 20
  warm chicken liver salad 82
  warm duck, shallot & orange salad 110
  warm mackerel & potato salad 144
  warm new potato & lentil salad 187
  warm oriental-style salad 250
  warm peach & goat cheese salad 303
  warm red lentil salad 206
  warm salmon & mango salad 137
watercress
  chicken & cranberry salad 312
  coronation chicken salad 70
  melon & mango salad 282
  salt chili squid salad 262
  smoked chicken salad 74
  smoked trout, endive & pear salad 138
  strawberry & watercress salad 298
  sweet & sour fish salad 149
  walnut, pear & crispy bacon salad 37
  watercress, zucchini & mint salad 235
watermelon
  fig & watermelon salad 292
  minted pea & melon salad 286
  spring clean salad 294
wild rice salad 202

yogurt
  broiled lamb with yogurt dressing 62
  cantaloupe & crab salad 291
  chicken & grapefruit salad 310
  chilled berry breakfast salad 268
  coronation chicken salad 70
  lamb kofte & herb salad 64
  layered chicken salad 68
  melon & mango salad 282
  melon & strawberry salad 285
  nutty beet salad 223
  pear & Roquefort salad 304
  red cabbage & beet slaw 214
  salad with garlic dressing 220
  smoked chicken salad 74
  sweet potato & bean salad 190
  warm red lentil salad 206
  warm salmon & mango salad 137
  watercress, zucchini & mint salad 235

zucchini
  layered chicken salad 68
  raspberry & feta salad 297
  roasted vegetable salad 172
  turkey couscous salad 104
  warm oriental-style salad 250
  watercress, zucchini & mint salad 235